David Leadbetter
Faults and *Fixes*

To Kelly, Andy and Hally –
your love and support inspire me to teach

David Leadbetter

Faults and *Fixes*

with John Huggan

Illustrations by
Dave F. Smith

Foreword by
Nick Price

CollinsWillow
An Imprint of HarperCollins*Publishers*

First published in 1993 by
Collins Willow
an imprint of HarperCollins*Publishers*
London

First published in
paperback in 1998

5   7   9   8   6   4

A CIP catalogue record for this book
is available from the British Library

ISBN 0 00 218838 4

Edited by Richard Simmons

Designed and produced by
Cooling Brown, Hampton, Middlesex

Printed in Hong Kong

CONTENTS

FOREWORD

I first met David Leadbetter at a junior tournament at Royal Harare in Zimbabwe, in 1968. I was eleven years old at the time and did not realize that he would go on to become one of the world's most successful and respected golf teachers.

During the mid-1970s, golf in our country hit an all-time high, and David, along with a good friend of ours, George Harvey (of whom Gerald Micklem, twice captain of the R&A, once said, "He may be one of the best amateurs I've ever seen"), spent countless hours together on the practice tee and in the clubhouse poring through golf instructional books and magazines. I believe it was at this time that David really began to see that his future in golf was rooted in teaching.

As long as I have known David, he has always had his nose buried in golf magazines, all the time learning, experimenting and never disputing any article until he had given it his full attention. Even if he didn't totally agree with what the author or article was implying, he would find something positive in it.

Having the ability to adapt to the student, along with simplifying the theories so that most of us can understand them, are David's strongest assets.

As with most great teachers, David has an uncanny knack of being able to get to the heart of any problem extremely quickly and, most importantly, he makes the student fully understand *why* he has a problem rather than just telling him to 'do it because I say so!'

In essence, David bases his theory on the simple premise that in order to consistently strike the ball well, the bigger muscles, ie. the trunk and legs, must control the smaller ones, ie. hands, wrists, and arms. 'The dog wags the tail', as he terms it. Not only does this method apply to the full swing but also to the short game and to putting on the green. Once learned, it all adds up to an enhanced sense of control and that, ultimately, is what golf is all about.

I like to look at my career so far as having two parts: The first part – pre-David Leadbetter – where I spent most of my time on the practice tee, experimenting and trying to find (through trial and error) something that would work consistently. That consistency, unfortunately, never lasted for more than a week or two.

The second part began in 1982, when I started working with David full time. There has been steady progress since then and, although it has been slow at times, I now feel I have a better understanding of my golf swing and game. When I practise, I am confident that I am improving all the time.

Fifteen years of David Leadbetter's experience and hard work are condensed in *Faults and Fixes*. It covers a variety of common problems that we golfers face. Whether you shoot in the 100s or in the 70s, I know this book will help you with its quick-and-easy suggestions to improve your game.

Nick Price

INTRODUCTION

The success of my first book, *The Golf Swing*, really amazed me. In the three years that it has been out, it has become one of the best-selling instruction books of all time, is now being published in eight different languages, and has provided a step-by-step plan for golfers of all abilities to build and develop an athletic golf swing.

In writing *The Golf Swing*, I dealt specifically with the theoretical aspects of the modern method of instruction. These theories were based on the knowledge I have accumulated through many years of working with some of the world's greatest players. As a full-time student of the game, *The Golf Swing* represented a golden opportunity to get wrapped up in one of my favorite subjects – swing theory. Call it a purist's dream.

Since its publication, *The Golf Swing* has become the cornerstone of the David Leadbetter Golf Academy teaching 'philosophy'. However, along with my team of certified teachers (who instruct at our growing number of academies around the world), I am fully aware that every golfer, no matter what his or her caliber, has problems that pertain to them personally. So, within the overall 'philosophy' that I work by, there remains plenty of room for flexibility to help individuals rid themselves of particular faults, or bad habits, and build a swing upon the basis of solid, proven fundamentals. Hence my enthusiasm to write *Faults and Fixes* – essentially a trouble-shooting manual which has been formulated to cover not only the full swing but a whole variety of faults and common problems associated with all aspects of the game.

Although it has taken over two years to complete, *Faults and Fixes* was an exciting project, and I am delighted that the book fulfills the objective of providing a comprehensive, fault-fixing guide for the benefit of everyone who just wants to play better golf. I believe that it demonstrates the versatility that my method of teaching offers; essentially a self-help manual for different players with many different problems – just as we encounter everyday with all of the pupils we teach around the world.

The experience of teaching thousands of different types of golfers has enabled me to identify certain faults that crop up frequently. I sincerely believe that, thanks to the clarity of the writing and the quality of the descriptive artwork, you will find many questions you have to ask about the game will be answered in a simple and straightforward manner.

There are 80 faults and 80 fixes in all. Some are a little easier to detect and eliminate than others. Indeed, in certain cases, having a friend watch you and (better still) video your swing will be a great asset. Knowing the fault is certainly key. However, a lot of the faults, which are easy to detect, can be fixed through having a greater knowledge of just what it takes to 'fix the fault'. It's a matter of trial and error.

How to make the most of Faults and Fixes

It has long been my belief that 'feel' plays a major part in accelerating the learning process. No matter what your level of play, being able to add a feeling to understanding is an invaluable asset; it's the best stepping stone that I know to improving your mechanics. To that end, the numerous drills and exercises that you will encounter throughout your reading will help you accelerate your improvement.

Most, if not all, of the common terms for faults that you have probably heard – ie. 'picking the club up', the 'reverse pivot', swinging over the top', 'casting the club' and so on – are listed at the end of this book in the Checklist (pp 190-192). As an exercise, I suggest that you first read through this checklist to try to find the fault or problems that you feel might most readily apply to you.

The full swing section (Section 1: Chapters One to Five) has been coded to assist you in locating your faults. Look in the top left-hand corner of each '*fault*' page and you will notice either 1, 2 or 3 golf balls as shown here:

● these faults usually (but not always) concern the better golfer
●● signifies a fault that most often applies to the average player
●●● in my experience these faults are universally applicable.

Consider this as nothing more than a general guide – some of the errors are applicable to other categories, and ultimately it's a case of matching the instruction to your own game.

To further enhance your understanding, I have highlighted what I consider to be the key aspects of each fix in bold text. Where it is helpful I have also made picture references in bold – ie. **(1), (2)** – to draw your attention to a particular detail in the illustration. Hopefully, this should enable you to get an instant visual idea of what your fault is – and, more importantly, just how to go about fixing it!

Some of the fixes might well come quickly to you – some you may have to work on for a while. But whatever the case, having a full understanding of the fault and a concise plan of action with which to eliminate it should inspire you to get out there and work on realizing your full potential as a golfer.

I hope that this book provides you with many hours of entertaining and enlightening reading – after all, you did help me to write it.

David Leadbetter, Florida, May 1993

CHAPTER 1
At Address

"Most swing errors can be traced to a poor set-up, so I regard the set-up as the most important fundamental in every athletic golf swing. The correct address position is designed to place the component parts of your body in a balanced state with the club prior to setting them in motion."

FAULT No.1

Poor positioning of the left hand

If there is one tip I could give the average golfer – especially slicers and those who lack distance – it would be to stress the importance of fitting his or her left hand on to the grip correctly.

As the first point of contact between the player and the club, the left hand represents the essential coupling that is required to hinge the wrists and get the club swinging freely. The problem is, a player's grip can be deceptive. What may look correct on the surface may conceal a can of worms beneath; you never really know until you open out the fingers for a look inside.

Take a closer look at your left hand grip. Holding the club as you would normally, open your hand and check the position of the club: if the shaft runs high across your palm **(1)**, then my bet is that the ability of your wrist to hinge correctly is greatly inhibited – a fault that probably costs you both distance and accuracy. A sure sign that you have this fault is a hole quickly worn through your glove on the fleshy pad at the heel of your hand **(2)** – so it costs you money, too.

(1)

(2)

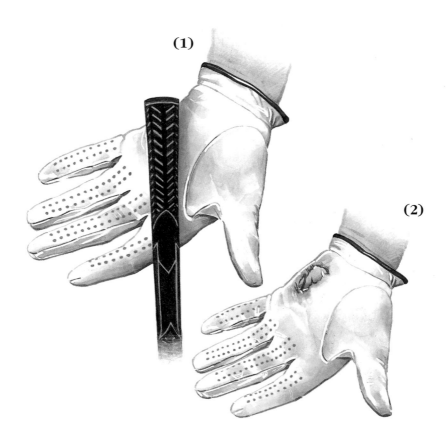

FIX NO.1

Learn to free-up the hinge

✓ From a free standing position, bend forwards – allowing your arms to hang freely in front of your body – and notice the way in which your palms naturally tend to point inwards. Now, maintaining this arm position, take a club and place it in your left hand, making sure that **the leading edge of the clubface and the back of your left forearm are parallel (1)**. As you do this, try to position your left thumb so that it points straight down the shaft, slightly to the right of centre, and also keep it **'short'** on the shaft. (In terms of creating leverage in your swing, a shorter thumb – as opposed to one that is fully extended – is much more effective.)

Having taken this new grip, hold the club out in front of you and look down at it. You should be able to see two to three knuckles on the back of your left hand **(2)**, and generally be aware of an increased sense of feel for the clubhead.

The real difference, however, lies within. Open your grip again and you'll see what I mean. This time the shaft should run diagonally from the base of your little finger through to the middle of your index finger **(3)**. Although still primarily a 'palm' grip, **you will sense that it's more in the fingers**. This improved hold on the club will increase the flexibility in your left wrist, and so **encourage the free-hingeing motion that is necessary to create the maximum clubhead speed through impact**.

(1)　　　　　　　**(2)**　　　　　　　**(3)**

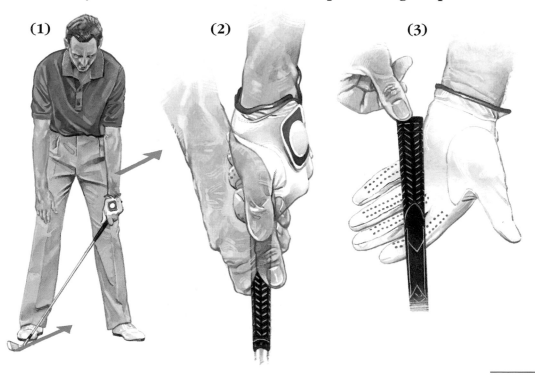

FAULT No.2

Poor positioning of the right hand

I believe that in every good golf swing the right and left sides of the body play equal parts – a symmetry that is best achieved when the hands work together in unison.

This poses a problem for many people who are naturally right-handed; they are inclined to grip the club too much in the palm of their right hand **(1)**, as if they were grabbing hold of a hammer. In other words, their right hand tends to dominate the left **(2)**.

Although such a hold on the club might induce a sense of power, it actually creates a series of problems which collectively render the swing power*less*. Not least of these problems is the fact that the club tends to be picked up almost exclusively by the right hand, which immediately destroys any hope of width and rhythm in the backswing. A jerky 'pick-up' also upsets the alignment of the clubface, and inevitably encourages excessive use of the upper body to hit at the ball from the top of the backswing.

To form an effective working union with the left hand, your right hand must be applied to the club in what we describe as a *neutral* position. Only then will you reap the benefit of a properly coordinated hand and body movement.

(1)　　　　　　　　　　　　**(2)**

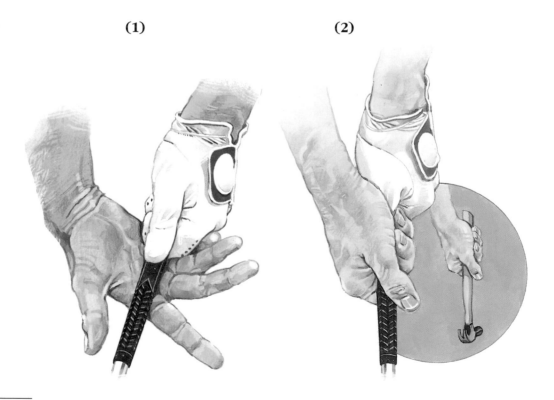

FIX No. 2

Grip the club more in the fingers

✓ For an improved sense of feel (and a better working relationship with the left hand), **the club should be held primarily in the fingers of the right hand**. The shaft should run diagonally from the base of your little finger through the joints of the second and third fingers and on to the middle of your index finger **(1)**. When you close your right hand the left thumb should then be totally covered, fitting snugly beneath the fleshy pad at the base of your right thumb.

In the completed grip, **check to see that your hands are parallel on the club (2)**. Also, there should be a slight gap between the index and second finger on your right hand. The index finger itself should be hooked around the grip in what's known as the 'trigger' position, its tip lightly touching the end of your right thumb. So placed, the right index finger and right thumb are responsible for much of the 'feel' in your right hand – **waggle the clubhead and you will quickly appreciate what I mean**.

Whether you prefer the overlapping grip **(3)**, or the less popular interlocking or ten-finger grip, this manner of placing the hands on the club will reduce the likelihood of 'snatching' the clubhead away, and instead **encourages the hands to work together**.

(1)   **(2)**   **(3)**

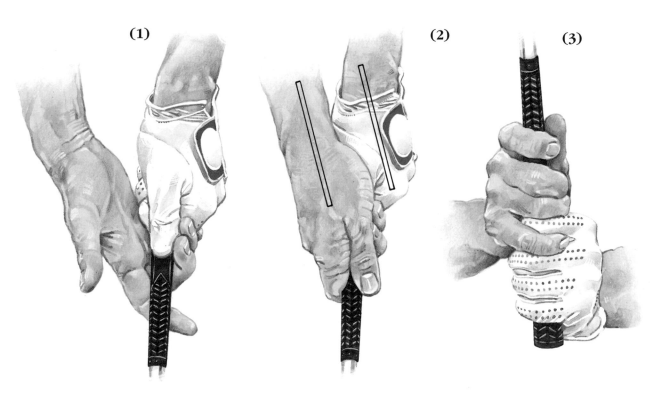

FAULT NO.3

Losing your grip during the swing

X Do you ever sense your hands coming off the club during your swing? If you do, you've got a serious problem. Any loosening of the hands will instinctively cause you to re-grip at some stage, which will almost inevitably disrupt the alignment of the clubface prior to impact. Where you hit the ball is then nothing but a lottery.

Losing control of the grip is most likely to occur at the top of the backswing, and is particularly prevalent amongst those players who are prone to overswinging. Generally speaking, the fault takes one of two common forms: either the fleshy part of the right hand becomes detached from the left thumb **(1)**, or the last three fingers on the left hand work loose of the butt-end of the grip **(2)**.

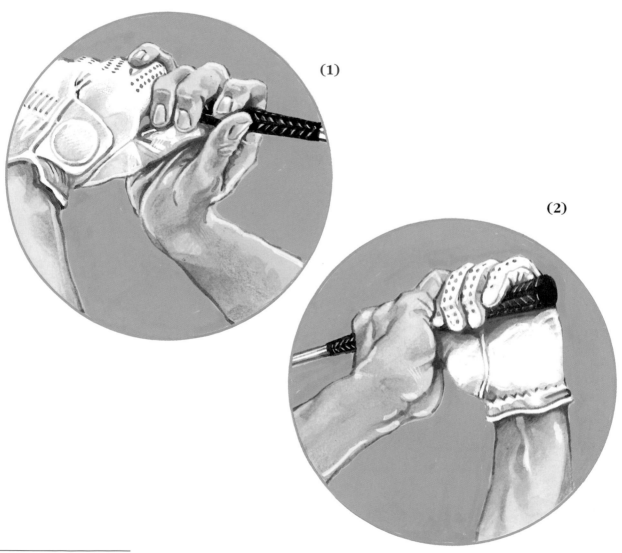

(1)

(2)

FIX NO.3

Firm up your key pressure points

No teacher worth his salt would ever recommend that you grip the club tightly. There are, however, **specific pressure points** that **should exist in order to maintain control**.

For example, at address, **the last three fingers** of your left hand should be wrapped fairly firmly around the butt-end of the club. Their job is to keep the left hand securely in place. You should also be aware of **a little pressure on your left thumb** as you place the lifeline of your right palm firmly upon it, and also **pressure of your right index finger** as it pushes against the shaft. That seals your grip perfectly.

There's an easy way to check that you maintain these pressure points throughout your swing – all you need are several long blades of grass. Place some between the fleshy heel of your left hand and the club **(1)**; the rest put on top of your left thumb, extended down the shaft, to be trapped beneath the fleshy part of your right hand **(2)**.

Once you've done that, prepare to hit some half shots with a wedge, **keeping your overall grip pressure constant** so that the grass stays in place **(3)**. Then, having completed your swing, check to see that your hands are in the same position they were in at address. As you work up to hitting full shots you'll soon begin to appreciate the value of 'hands-on' control.

(1)

(2)

(3)

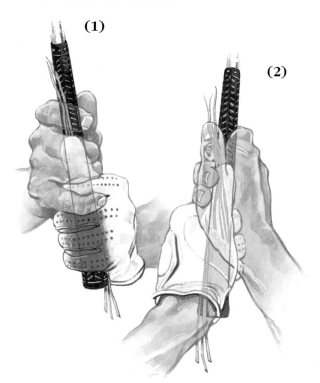

FAULT NO.4

Poor posture at address

 As a teacher I try to keep golf a simple game, but I'm afraid it's time for a simple geometry lesson – and the subject is 'body angles'.

Of all the angles we can identify in the golf swing, I believe it is those you create at address that are most important. Indeed, the quality of your 'static' position at the set-up pretty much determines the quality of your body motion and your balance. If your angles are correct to begin with, you'll find it a lot easier to maintain them throughout your swing. A sound posture is therefore a prerequisite for good golf.

Unfortunately, too many amateurs try to run with their laces tied: I see players stoop from the waist, others slouch their backs, some overly flex or straighten their legs, and many appear to have had their chins glued to their chest in a futile effort to 'keep their head down'. If any of this sounds familiar, you have virtually no chance of making a good swing. But don't feel bad about it. The best players in the world occasionally struggle with their posture. In fact, nine times out of ten it's a faulty body position at address that causes their games to go sour.

Fix No.4

Create and maintain good angles

The following exercise should be performed initially without a club – we'll start with your general body position. To begin, stand erect, then turn your feet outwards slightly (for most clubs, the distance between your heels should be no greater than the width of your shoulders). Now **flex your knees a little until** you can feel your weight moving forward on to the arches of your feet; **stick your rear end out** – keeping your lower back straight – **and keep your chin up**.

Looking good so far. Now let your arms hang down as if holding a club, and feel **your upper arms resting lightly on your chest**. Finally, tilt your left hip and left shoulder up slightly, and at the same time relax your right side, dropping your right shoulder just a fraction.

That's it. Your **spine angle** and **centre of gravity** are now correctly positioned. If it feels awkward, it's probably correct. Check your posture regularly in a mirror, and compare your body position with that of the pro's on TV. With a little practice, you can look as good as they do.

FAULT No.5

Misalignment of clubface at address

This may sound obvious, but firing a ball at a target is made a lot easier if you set up with the clubface aimed squarely at that target to begin with. Obvious, maybe. Easy to achieve? Not necessarily.

The problem in golf is that you are forced to stand to the side of the ball in order to hit it, and as a result your eyes can often fool you into thinking the clubface is squarely aligned to the target, when in fact it isn't. And when you make the mistake of aiming the clubface in the wrong direction, you have no choice but to compromise your swing to get the ball flying on line. And that only leads to trouble.

Generally speaking, players who set up with the clubface aiming to the right of their target **(1)** tend to hook the ball. And the more they hook it, the more they aim off to the right to compensate. The same applies to those who slice. In order to offset a severe left-to-right ball flight, they set up with the clubface aimed more and more to the left of their target **(2)**. Either way, a lack of consistency will result.

(1)   **(2)**

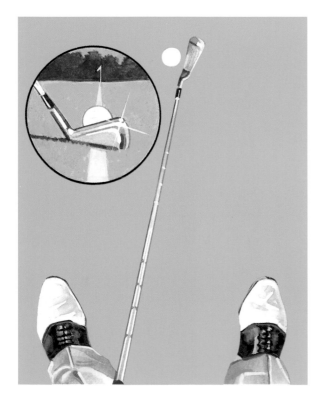
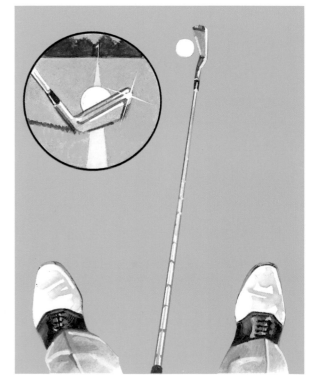

FIX No.5

'Square' your clubface in one easy move

Try this simple exercise for better clubface alignment at address. First, place a club on the ground, pointing directly at your target. Then, having adopted your normal stance and grip, hold a second club up waist high in front of you, making sure that the **leading edge is vertical,** ie. pointing up towards 12 o'clock – **the clubface perfectly 'square' (1).**

The next step requires precision: without changing the angle of the face in any way, lower the clubhead so that **the leading edge forms a perfect right angle with the shaft you laid on the ground (2)**. (If this looks strange, you have obviously been guilty of misaligning your clubface for some time.)

Repeat this exercise a number of times, then take it a stage further: replace the second shaft with a ball, and attempt to hit some shots. Trust that the face is square, even if at first the ball flies off-line. You'll adjust instinctively to the correction. And when you do, clubface alignment is one less aspect of the set up you'll have to worry about.

(1)   **(2)**

FAULT No.6

Misalignment of body at address

X Aiming a golf club isn't like aiming a rifle, where you have the luxury of looking straight down the barrel at the target. When you set up to play a golf shot your body is positioned to the left of the ball, forcing you to look down the target line at something of an angle. And that's not always easy to reconcile.

Basically, there are two ways in which you can go wrong. Some players aim their feet at the target – which in itself is a mistake – then compound the error by paying little attention to the alignment of their hips, shoulders or, indeed, the clubface. Others simply offset their alignment to compensate for an existing fault in their swing. Someone swinging from out-to-in with an open clubface, for example, will usually slice the ball. After firing a few shots into the right-hand woods he soon figures out that if he aims further to the left he can at least play with his slice. 'A fault to fix a fault', you might say.

So it's really a case of which comes first, the chicken or the egg; is poor alignment causing a poor swing, or vice versa? Whichever it is, you need to rebuild your swing with the benefit of solid fundamentals – and one of those is a properly aligned body at address.

Fix No.6

Remember the rule of parallel alignment

☑ One of the easiest ways to grasp the principle of square alignment is to imagine that you are hitting a shot along a railway track. Picture yourself aiming the clubface at the target along the right hand rail, placing your feet parallel to that line, on the inner track. **Every part of your body – your eyes, shoulders, hips, knees – should be set parallel to your toe line (1)**. The same principle applies as lining up a 1-foot putt – the putter-face looks directly at the hole; your feet and body are aligned parallel left of the hole.

To groove this square body position, rehearse lining up next to a wall, or on perpendicular lines on your carpet at home. Out on the practice range, lay a club on the ground along your toe line to represent the inside track. Then use that as your guide.

By the way, you'll find it a lot easier to maintain this square alignment if, when viewing your target, you **learn to swivel your head so that your eyes look 'under' the play line (2)**. Make the mistake of lifting your head to check your line and you run the risk of altering your upper body alignment.

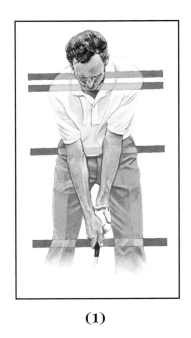

(1)

(2)

FAULT NO.7

Misalignment – for the better player

☒ Good players, no matter what their technique, instinctively find ways of hitting the ball towards the target. But they do so at a price; the more compensations they are forced to employ, the more likely their swing is to succumb to pressure. So although a good player may live with his faults, if his swing is fundamentally flawed, he will probably never realize his true potential.

Generally speaking, the good player's bad shot usually flies to the left. To compensate for this he instinctively closes his stance, thus aligning his body to the right of his target **(1)**. Such a misaligned set-up tends to set the right shoulder in a very low, submissive position, which in turn shifts his eyeline even further to the right of the target, and places his head too far behind the ball **(2)**.

From here, the player must either pull the ball back on line, or actively employ his hands to square the clubface through impact. This he may well be able to do, but both options require perfect timing, and neither can be relied upon.

(1)   **(2)**

FIX NO.7

Make room for a free, uninhibited release

☑ If your tendency is to consistently hit shots left, I want you to aim more to the left, not right; I want you to get used to the feeling of setting up with more of an open stance, so that you **give yourself the room that is necessary to release the club freely down the target line as your body rotates through impact**.

Try this simple routine: standing with your chest open in relation to the target line, set up to the ball with just your right hand on the club **(1)**. Then, leaving the right side of your body where it is, place your left hand on the grip **(2)**. You should now feel 'lopsided', as if you were playing downhill and aiming way off to the left. But don't worry, that exaggeration stems from the fact that this new position is so markedly different from your old one.

In reality, your shoulders are more level and your right forearm is set a little higher. Your knees, hips and eyes should now accord with the parallel alignment of the clubface; in other words, your body is set **'parallel left' of the ball-to-target line (3)**. Remember, it only *feels* open.

When you first practise from this position it will probably feel as if the ball will fly even further left than normal. But persevere. Keep your hands passive, and your instincts will quickly enable you to hit the ball straight at the target without any further manipulation.

(1)  **(2)**  **(3)**

FAULT NO.8

Poor ball position

This has probably happened to you: you're playing badly and your partner offers the suggestion that the ball is either too far back or too far forward in your stance. He may be correct, but treat his advice with caution. Your ball position may be a result of compensating for a poor swingpath, and so simply changing it might not do the trick. What may be the correct ball position for him is not necessarily what's best for you. Everyone is different, but generally speaking, a good player doesn't want the ball positioned too far back in his stance, and a high-handicapper shouldn't play it too far forward.

Let's take the example of the good player who is swinging the club excessively from in-to-out through impact (ie. creating a very shallow angle of attack). Tired of repeatedly hitting hooks and/or pushed shots or thinned shots, he will instinctively move the ball back in his stance to accommodate his faulty swingpath **(1)**. That's the only way he can hit the ball solidly.

A similar solution is usually sought by the player who swings steeply across the ball from out-to-in. The itinerant slicer generally feels more comfortable with the ball moved forwards in his stance **(2)**; it's the only way he can get by with his fundamental swing flaw.

So it could be argued that your ball position merely reflects the way you are swinging at a particular time. Having said that, it is possible to hit some good shots with such compensations built into your game. But I always feel that good fundamentals eventually pay off.

(1)   **(2)**

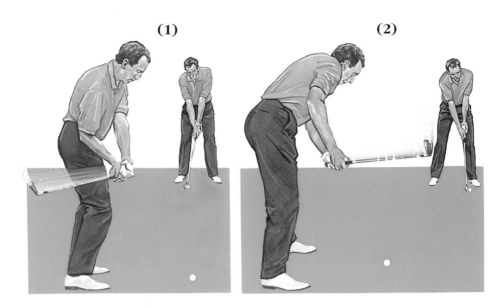

Fix No.8

Thoughts on a better ball position

Let me warn you up front that these corrections must normally be made in pairs. A slicer who moves the ball back in his stance will also have to work on getting his clubhead approaching the ball from the inside track. Only when he achieves both will his slice disappear altogether.

The same applies to the player who is constantly fighting a hook. Moving the ball forward in his stance will only help matters if at the same time he is able to work on improving his swingpath too, so that the club is more on line as it approaches the ball.

In each of these cases, the quality of the strike and the flight pattern of your shots is likely to be somewhat erratic during the initial stages of change. But stick with it. In the long run, the fewer swing compensations you are forced to make, the more consistent you will be.

Use this as your guide: a low handicap player (blue ball) who tends to use his lower body more aggressively should place the ball about **opposite the left heel when hitting a wood; and up to a couple of ball widths back of that point for an iron**. A higher handicapper (red ball) should put the ball in the middle of his stance when hitting an iron; **a little forward of that for a wood**. These rough guidelines should enable you to make a crisp, descending blow with an iron, and create more of an upward, sweeping motion with a wood.

FAULT NO.9

Stance too wide

X For some reason, I find that club golfers who use too wide a stance far outnumber those who play with their feet too close together. A possible explanation could be that many players associate a wide stance with greater stability and power. That's a mistake.

The reality of the situation is that a wide stance only serves to inhibit the free motion and transfer of your weight; furthermore it breeds tension in your lower body, and as a result over-involves the upper body in the striking of the ball. In short, there is no harmony between the feet, legs, arms and trunk, which forces you to hit *at* the ball rather than make a fluid swinging motion *through* the ball.

FIX NO.9

Narrow your stance for stability and mobility

The general rule of thumb here is your stance should be wide enough to enable you to maintain good balance, and yet narrow enough so you can shift your weight and rotate your body freely.

Of course, the width of your stance will vary according to the club you are using. For the majority of the longer shots you play – say, between a 5-iron and a driver – **I suggest strongly that you make sure that your heels are no further apart than the width of your shoulders (1)**. As for the shorter clubs, you must gradually narrow your stance as the length of the shaft decreases.

Once your stance has been narrowed to an acceptable level, **your footwork and lower body motion will feel more lively and improve dramatically (2)**, **as indeed will the overall rhythm and balance of your swing, and, of course, your ball striking (3)**.

(1)   **(2)**   **(3)**

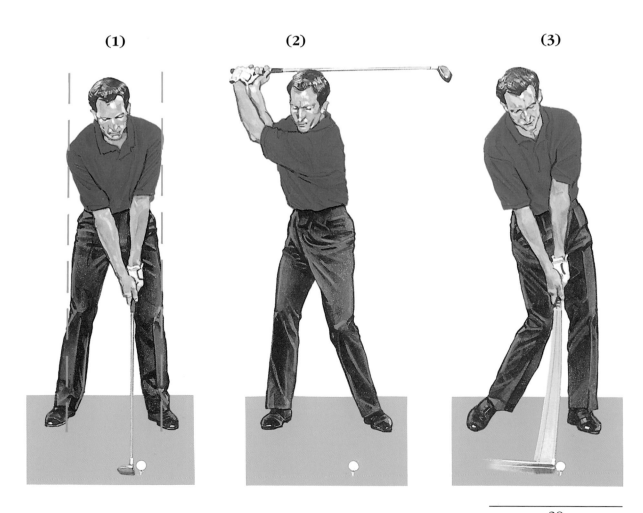

FAULT NO.10

Tension at address

X Every golfer has felt this at sometime or another: you're over the ball, but you're not sure about something. You're asking yourself questions: "Do I have the right club? Am I aiming in the right place? How much should I allow for the wind? What did I do wrong with that last shot?". Combine all this with tips and technical swing thoughts and you will suffer with '*paralysis through analysis*'.

The point is this: when your mind is cluttered, your body usually reacts by tensing up. This is especially noticeable at address, in the arms, in the shoulders and in the neck. Test yourself: grip a club normally, and hold it out in front of your body. If you can sense the weight of the clubhead in your hands, you're fine. If you cannot, then you're too 'tight', and the tension is sure to spread through your whole body and affect the rhythm of your swing.

FIX NO.10

Clap, relax, and free up your swing

Tension is a killer; it destroys any hope you may have of making a fluid swing. That's why it's so important that your mind is focused, and your body relaxed as you stand over a shot.

Be careful, though. To 'relax' does not equate with gripping the club loosely. After all, isn't it possible to shake someone firmly by the hand and yet still keep your arm relaxed? So it should be with the golf club. **Shake hands with the grip**, **but keep those arms 'soft'**.

Let's get the proper feel. Without a club, stand as if you were going to hit a shot. Let your arms hang limply in front of your body, then swing your arms and clap your palms together **(1)**. Do it again. And again – sensing a **'heaviness'** in your arms. Any lingering tension in your arms and shoulders should disappear. Now grip a club and try to reproduce that same relaxed feeling in your **upper body, while being aware of a lightness in your feet and legs down below** – just as if you were standing on thin ice **(2)**.

Swing the club initially in slow motion, and once you have enhanced your feeling of **softness**, and can **feel the weight of the clubhead**, swing at normal speed, and hit some full shots. Be aware also of keeping your chin up as a further guard against tension in your shoulders. Remember, **the more relaxed your body is, the more rhythmic your swing will be, and the more clubhead speed you'll be able to produce**.

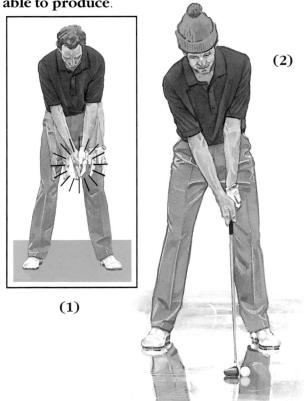

(2)

(1)

FAULT NO.11

Poor mental picture of the swing

X Good players tend to make the swing look easy; the majority of club golfers, sadly, do not. Often, their problem is that they work on their swing piecemeal, without ever really having a clear mental picture of what the finished product should actually look like. Not that it isn't important to be aware of certain positions within your swing; it is. But focusing on 'bits' can make it difficult to link the many component parts into one continuous flowing motion. So the simpler the image, the better.

If you are one of the countless golfers whose idea of hitting the ball revolves around such thoughts on the backswing as 'move the arms and the body will follow', or on the downswing 'shift the weight and the club will follow', or 'roll the hands open and then closed', then it's time to clear your mind. What you need is to develop a much clearer picture of the overall swing.

Fix No. 11

Turn in a barrel; swing along the rim

✓ **There are two basic components in the swing – (1) the trunk**, which is supported by the legs and feet, and (2) **the unit of the arms, hands and club**. Now, here's the concept I want you to visualize. As the first component (your trunk) turns and rotates on a fairly horizontal plane, the second component (your arms and the club) swings on a comparatively vertical plane. (Think of the trunk as being the engine, the hub of the swing around which the arms and the club move in a circular fashion.)

Although it's not an entirely accurate analogy, a good way to grasp this notion is to imagine **your trunk turns within the confines of a barrel**, **while the club moves up and down along the rim of a wheel.** So, as your body rotates to the right, the clubhead moves up along the rim of the wheel to the top of the backswing; then, as your body rotates back to the left, the club moves down the rim of the wheel and up once again as you complete your follow-through (in effect, a mirror-image of the backswing).

Of course, in reality the swing is not a perfect circle, as the dynamics of the motion require the club to change planes. Nor does your body rotate in a precise circular fashion; to facilitate the correct weight shift there also has to be a slight lateral movement involved. Nevertheless, the barrel-and-wheel concept should help to improve your understanding of the golf swing, and as a result will encourage the major components in your swing to work together in harmony.

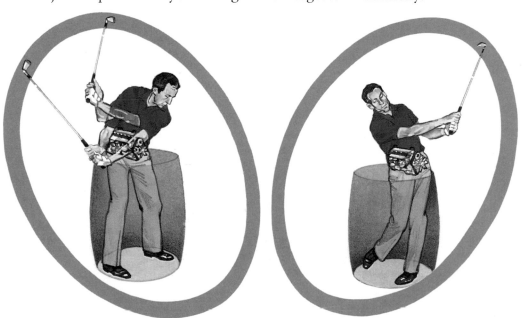

CHAPTER 2
The Backswing

"A good basic backswing demands the
synchronized movement of the club,
hands, arms and torso. Sequencing
these moves correctly will set off the
proper chain reaction in order to
facilitate a powerful move back
to the ball."

FAULT NO.12

'Picking the club up'

X I have always been of the opinion that the concept of 'hit' in golf is a very dangerous one. Whenever a player's focus shifts away from simply *swinging* the clubhead to forcibly *hitting* the ball, problems are never too far behind.

One of these problems is a tendency to use the hands excessively in the process of moving the club away from the ball. Using the hands to start the swing usually results in the clubhead being picked up off the ground far too abruptly. Hence the observation: 'the problem with his swing is that he is picking the club up'.

Perhaps given the fact that one takes hold of the club with the hands, that the ball is stationary, and that it is the golfer's natural instinct to try to help the ball into the air, this is hardly surprising. However, such a fault only leads to a narrowing of the swing arc and a steep, choppy downswing – neither of which you should welcome.

FIX NO.12

Start right – sweep away a second ball

The first move away from the ball is crucial; it determines the shape and tempo of your entire swing. Here's an image that might help you. At address, think of your arms and shoulders as forming an inverted isosceles triangle. Then, **to make a smooth, one-piece 'moveaway', focus on turning this triangle back with your chest and navel (1)**. **Sense that you control the movement of your arms and the club with the bigger muscles in your shoulders and trunk**, and maintain the shape of the triangle until your hands are opposite your right leg. **Moving the club, hands, arms, chest and shoulders away together as a unit will start the clubhead away low and your backswing will be full and wide**. Just as it should be.

To check that you move the club away correctly, place a second ball about a foot behind your object ball – just inside the ball-to-target line – and try to sweep it away smoothly as your 'triangle' moves the club back **(2)**. When you do that you know the clubhead has travelled low to the ground and on the correct path. Hit shots as you perform this drill; the practice will give you the confidence to trust your new, wide moveaway out on the course.

(1)

(2)

FAULT NO.13

Clubhead moves inside too quickly

X A good start to your swing gives you a fair chance of hitting a good shot; a poor start reduces the odds considerably. Bad starts come in many guises, but one of the most common is dragging the clubhead inside (or behind you) too quickly.

This fault can usually be traced to a simple misinterpretation of one of two cliches: 'turn away from the ball', or 'swing from in-to-out'. The first of these causes you to turn your body aggressively early in the backswing; the second encourages you to exaggerate the 'in' part of your backswing, in the mistaken belief that this will help you swing 'in-to-out' on the downswing.

Whatever the reason, an exaggerated inside move will either create a very flat swing, or more often force you to lift your arms very steeply in order to get the club to the top of the backswing. Not only does this ruin a good body turn, but in the case of the 'in-to-out' player, it actually encourages the opposite motion – ie. an 'out-to-in' loop.

FIX NO.13

Butt-end in; clubhead out

Let me explain the precise nature of the moveaway. During the first few feet of your swing, the clubhead should move gradually inside the ball-to-target line. But at the same time it must also stay **'outside' your hands**. (The path along which the clubhead moves is thus closer to the ball-to-target line than the path that is taken by the hands – as indicated in the illustration). This clubhead/hands relationship sets the club on the proper plane, and encourages your arms and body to move in unison all the way to the top of the backswing.

The key to getting this move right lies in initiating the swing with the butt-end of the club, as opposed to the clubhead. Moving the butt in towards your right thigh will help you to keep the clubhead outside your hands, and gets it started on the correct path. For the habitual out-to-in swinger, **this much straighter moveaway will encourage the club to drop down on to the correct inside path from the top of the backswing.**

FAULT NO.14

Taking the clubface back closed

X As I have stated previously, the fewer compensations you are forced to make in your swing to hit the ball on line, the better it will be. So as a teacher who likes to keep the swing relatively simple, I try as far as possible to help golfers eliminate certain fundamental errors which force them to make such a compromise.

Take the example of the player who tends to close the clubface early in the swing (ie. turns the clubface counter-clockwise). Now I'm not saying that it isn't possible to play some good golf with a closed clubface. It is. But it's more difficult. In order to square the face at impact, the player must somehow learn to manipulate the clubhead at some later stage in the swing, and to do that consistently will require many hours of practice. The point is, why put yourself through all that hard work?

If your shots are inconsistent, and you suspect that you may be guilty of closing the clubface early in your swing, try this simple test: from your address position, move the club away from the ball until your hands reach a point opposite the middle of your right thigh **(1)**. Now shuffle your whole body around and face the clubhead **(2)**: if it appears to be in the same position it was in at address, then it's square. But if the toe is ahead of the heel **(inset)**, it's already closed.

(1)   **(2)**

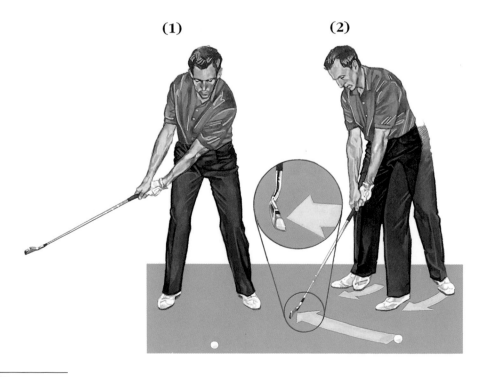

Fix No.14

Rotate the clubface as you turn

☑ First, check your grip as covered in Faults No. 1 and No. 2. A fundamental problem here may cause a closed clubface.

Secondly, try this for a simple piece of mental imagery: from the address position, **think of the clubface as a gate which opens slowly in conjunction with the turning motion of your body.** Now focus on your left arm – as you rotate it gently clockwise in the moveaway, note the effect this has on the clubface **(1)**; as it opens gradually, see how it remains square in relation to your body. (As you do this, **make sure that you keep your arms and hands soft**.)

Here's another drill that will help you to achieve a neutral clubface position in the moveaway. Fix a tee so that it points straight out of the little gap between the velcro and the leather on the back of your glove. This will help you to observe the rotation of your left arm and left hand. Now, as you rehearse your initial moveaway from the ball, your goal is to make the tee point straight ahead and the toe of the club point straight upwards as the shaft approaches the horizontal **(2)**.

Practise getting that right, then hit some shots. You'll probably leave the ball out to the right at first, but work at it. Before long you'll have a much more orthodox clubface position, and as a result hit more straight shots.

(1)   **(2)**

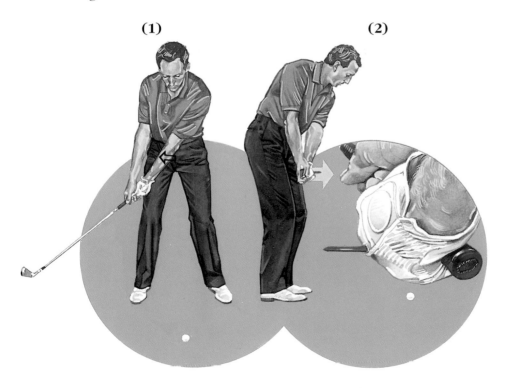

FAULT NO. 15

Flat, laid-off backswing

X When an amateur describes a swing as being 'flat', he is usually referring to the plane of the left arm at the top of the backswing. That plane, however, can be deceiving.

The trouble with a player's swingplane is that it can change dramatically between the halfway stage (where it could be flat) and the top of the backswing (where it could be upright). Reversing the process, what you see at the top is therefore not necessarily representative of the real fault. That's why I look no further than to the halfway position to get to the root of any backswing problem.

Generally, if at the halfway stage in your backswing the grip end of the club points at the ball-to-target line (or beyond), you are too flat, or 'laid-off'. (Quick check: with the club pointing behind you at such a low angle, the clubhead will feel very heavy. It's out of balance.)

This fault often stems from a misunderstanding of such swing thoughts as 'take the club inside', or 'tuck the right elbow into the side'. Fanning or rotating the clubface open too much in the moveaway is another possible cause. Any one – or any combination – of these misleading swing thoughts has the potential to put you in a severely laid-off position halfway back.

Fix No.15

Check your plane halfway back

By the time you reach the halfway stage in your backswing, your goal is to have the club 'in balance', so that it can work in harmony with the turning of your body. In this position your left arm should be 'snug' to your body; your right elbow splayed out slightly, and your wrists fully cocked. Try this drill.

Take a mid-iron, and choke down to the bottom of the grip. Swing the club back to halfway, hingeing the wrists and keeping your left arm lightly on your chest. **Make sure that your left elbow points down towards the ground**. That assists the upward movement of the club and counteracts any excess rotation of the left arm. **The grip-end of the club should now be pointing at a spot about midway between your feet and the ball.**

Now, can you feel how much lighter the club feels at this point? That's because you have 'set' the club correctly; it's in balance. If you have suffered with a severely laid-off backswing for some time, then this correct position will feel overly upright. But trust it – it's perfectly on plane. And from here completing the backswing is easy. Just keep turning and you'll swing the club into a solid position at the top.

FAULT NO.16

Body turn completed too early

X If you suffer with this problem – and many good players do – the only way that you'll really begin to understand it is to view your swing in slow motion on a video screen. Then you'll see how certain parts of your body – either the hips, shoulders, or both – complete their rotation and coil long before your arms have reached their highest point in the swing. (In the illustration below, see how full the body turn is, yet the arms are only halfway back.) You will see on video how the arms will move independently of the turn for several frames to reach the top. In short, your backswing is out of 'sync'.

As a result of this 'early-turn syndrome', the all-important linkage between the arms and body is ruined. Inevitably, the same is true on the downswing. The trunk of your body again gets too far ahead of the action, and the hands and arms have to somehow 'race' to catch up if you are to hit the ball consistently.

Fix No.16

Coordinate the turning elements

Although it doesn't quite happen this way, think of your arms and body completing the backswing motion at exactly the same time. To achieve that, **the right side of your body must control the amount of turn that takes place in the early part of your swing; it needs to provide a certain resistance to slow the rotation of your knees, hips and shoulders**.

That resistance will not only serve to restrict the amount of early body turn you are able to make, but will also make it much easier for your arms and club to move away in 'sync' with your torso (which is the engine that powers your swing). Check your movements again on video: halfway back there should be substantially less body-turn. From this position, **the big muscles in your trunk can now complete the backswing motion in tandem with your arms**.

You'll get the idea with this simple drill: from address, take your right hand off the club, and let it hang in front of you. Now push the club back a short distance, letting your left arm pass underneath your right arm. Feel the resistance? Once you do, put your right hand back on the club and complete your backswing.

You should now sense a completely different blending of your arms and body. **Everything's working in 'sync'** and, as a result, your downswing will be better coordinated, too. Your hands, arms and body will release 'together' – there's no catching up required.

CHAPTER 3
At the Top

"The correct synchronizing of the pivot
action of the body and the swinging
motion of the arms, hands and club will
place the club in a consistent slot at the
top of the swing – readying it for the
journey down to impact."

FAULT NO.17

Reverse hip tilt

X In a good swing, the powerful coiling of the upper body blends effortlessly with the supportive action of the legs. The harmony of this overall motion is pretty much dependent on the movement of the hips. If the hips fail to move correctly, the player is often forced to lean his upper body heavily to the right in order to get his weight onto his right side. When that happens his left hip and left buttock shift precariously toward the target as his body rotates to complete the backswing.

The result is a classic 'reverse hip tilt', where the player does not get fully 'loaded' and his upper body is simply too far behind the lower body, clearly illustrated by the size of the gap between the left shoulder and the left hip. In effect, the upper body has moved too much off the ball and the angle of the spine is too tilted away from the vertical. This position at the top of the swing can result in poor synchronization of the arms and the body on the downswing.

Fix No.17

'Bump' to the right

☑ Ideally, at the top of the backswing your upper body should have turned on top of your lower body. That's what creates dynamic tension and a powerful coil. Here's how you achieve it: from the address position, you need to introduce a tiny amount of **lateral** movement before your hips begin to rotate. That's the key. You must learn to ease your hips to the right just a fraction before you start to turn.

To measure this, you need a point of reference. Stick an umbrella in the ground just outside your right foot, and angle it toward you just a little. Now, as you start your swing, shift your weight across so that you **bump the umbrella with your right hip (1)**; it's exactly that – a 'bump', not a sway to the right. Now complete your turn **(2)**. At the top you should find that you have moved away from the umbrella again. In the correct position you should feel more 'centred' at the top of the backswing – **both the upper and lower halves of your body now more closely in line, the spine closer to vertical**.

This simple exercise will give you the proper feel: making sure that your left knee resists a little, hold your left hip with your right hand and pull it in and across. You'll feel your hips more underneath you.

(1)   (2)

FAULT NO.18

Incomplete body turn

X The powerful turning/winding action of the body is a common factor in any good swing. Incorporating a full turn and weight shift, the athletic body pivot creates the torque that's necessary to hit the ball solidly. And that's what you must strive to achieve.

The trouble is, not everyone is comfortable with such a liberal use of the body in the swing. Many players, particularly those who have been lectured on the perils of 'swaying', and keeping the head still, are actually afraid of the motion that's involved in making a full turn. Their feeling is that the more they turn away from the target, the more likely they are to mishit the ball. They are wrong. A good swing, by definition, involves the use of your whole body. If your hips and shoulders fail to play their part, your arms are forced to take over the responsibility of getting the club to the top of the backswing. The result? You end up in a very weak, arms-orientated backswing position – one with little or no coil, and thus no energy stored to accelerate the clubhead through impact.

FIX NO.18

Feel the benefit of a full turn

Here's how to really feel your turn. In front of a mirror, take your address position, then place your hands on your hips and turn to the right, as if you were looking at someone standing directly behind you **(1)**. Can you **feel the rotation of your spine** and the coil and torsion that simple move creates?

Now take a look in the mirror. See how **your back faces the target** – your shoulders having turned through at least 90 degrees, your hips about half that amount **(2)**. Make a note, too, that your left knee points inward and that your weight is predominantly on your right side – specifically the inside of your right foot. That's crucial. You don't ever want to move onto the outside of your right foot. Work on this drill regularly – it will help you to build a much more powerful backswing turn. (If you find that you need to raise your left heel a little in order to complete your turn, then that's okay.) When you are familiar with the sensations involved, try hitting some shots. You'll be amazed at the difference in your ball-striking once you learn to trust your new turn.

(1)   **(2)**

FAULT NO.19

Out of position right knee

One fundamental that I stress to all players, no matter what their ability, is the need to coil into the right knee in the process of making a backswing. The right knee is the anchor which resists the powerful winding of your trunk. Any straightening or collapsing of the right leg lessens this resistance, and will generally produce a poor turn and a variety of bad shots.

Two basic errors are common: **(1)** a locking of the right knee so that the left knee shoots out towards the ball; and **(2)** a buckling of the right knee, where the player's weight moves on to the outside of the right foot – ie. a sway. As you can see, neither of the resulting backswing positions suggests consistency at impact.

(1)   **(2)**

FIX No.19

Flex your right knee, then coil against it

☑ Focus on the position of your right knee. Then, as you swing the club back, **try to retain the flex that you created in that knee at address all the way to the top of your backswing (1)**. (A feeling of **sitting down** on your right knee might help you to achieve this.)

You should now be aware of some 'athletic tension' in your right thigh. That's good. Any sensation of pressure in your right knee and thigh is a positive sign that you have offset any tendency to bow that knee outwards, as swayers are often inclined to do. (Quick check: with the help of a mirror positioned immediately to your right, look to see that your left knee does not shoot out towards the ball – there should be no daylight visible between your legs at the top of your swing.)

As an exercise, turn your right foot a few degrees inward at address, then make some swings **(2)**. You will immediately sense resistance in your right knee as your right leg anchors the swing. Loading up your backswing in this manner will create tremendous power; power you can unleash through the ball on the downswing.

(1)

(2)

FAULT NO. 20

Reverse pivot/poor weight transfer

X The transfer of weight is a fundamental element of any swinging motion. In golf, it's vital in the process of creating momentum.

From a fairly even distribution at address, your weight must be encouraged to shift onto the right leg on the backswing, and then onto the left leg for the follow-through. In other words, it must follow the natural progression of your body pivot, moving first away from and then towards the target.

In the case of the player who is inclined to make what is termed a 'reverse pivot', however, the opposite happens. Obsessed with thoughts of keeping the head down and left arm rigidly straight, the player's weight remains steadfast on his left side as he makes the backswing, resulting in the weight shifting back on to his right side on the downswing. Disaster! The proper turning motion of his body is now so restricted that his arms and hands have to play a big part in hitting the ball. The result? Total loss of power and accuracy.

FIX NO.20

Free-up your head, encourage your rotation

✓ **Allowing your head to turn to the right as you swing the club back encourages your spine to rotate, and gets your weight moving in the right direction**.

In the proper backswing movement, your left shoulder should then turn comfortably beneath your chin, so that your chest is aligned more on top of your right knee. As long as you keep your left arm 'soft' and relaxed, you should find that you swing easily into a powerful position at the top **(1)**. (A good tip to get the hang of this is to look at the ball out of your left eye at the top of the swing.) Take a look in a mirror. It doesn't look as bad as it feels, does it?

At first you may feel as if you are swaying, or moving off the ball, but don't worry about it. As long as your weight remains supported on the inside of your right foot, you're OK. Test yourself: at the top of your backswing, try to lift your left foot off the ground for a fraction of a second. If you can do this fairly easily, your weight is moving correctly. If you can't, you are still reverse-pivoting.

As an exercise, try one of my favourite drills. Adopt your address position, then place a club across your shoulders. As you turn back allow your head and spine to rotate and sense your balance **(2)**. Do this drill as often as you can. And when you think you've got it down...**keep doing it**.

(1)

(2)

FAULT NO.21

Overswinging – the case of the bent left arm

X Unless you are incredibly flexible, it is my opinion that you should never swing the club past the horizontal position at the top of your backswing. Anything longer than that is simply inefficient.

Generally speaking, apart from the obvious case of trying to hit the ball too hard, resulting in the swing getting out of control, there are two main causes of overswinging: (1) losing control of your grip on the club at the top (which I discussed in Fault No.3), and more commonly, (2) losing the natural width, or radius, of your backswing arc as a result of the right arm not working correctly.

At first glance, the sight of a severely bent left arm at the top would appear to explain a typical overswing, but that is misleading. The poor position of the left arm is merely indicative of an out-of-position right arm. The right arm controls the width of the swing – if the angle of the gap between the upper and lower arm (as shaded) is less than 90 degrees, an overswing will result.

Such an overswing is often accompanied by a lack of effective coiling in the torso, and inevitably produces inconsistent results. Thus, the key to shortening your swing is to first re-establish the width of your backswing arc.

FIX NO.21

The right angle for better extension

✓ To achieve the width that characterizes a good backswing **you must encourage your right elbow to work in such a way that as it folds, it forms a right angle – or 'L' shape – at the top**.

An image that might help you get into this position is to imagine that you are standing within a door frame, and that you swing your hands into the top right-hand corner of the door. Your left arm should be 'comfortably straight' (not tense), your right elbow positioned at 90 degrees, and, assuming your wrists hinge correctly, the clubshaft should lie along the top of the frame. Try it, and check your position in a mirror.

The 'split-grip' drill is another useful way to train your backswing **(inset)**. Split your hands a few inches apart on the grip, then swing the club back and push your right arm away to form that 90 degree angle at the elbow. (In a typical overswing the left arm tends to separate from the body too early, so as you make the backswing, feel that you exert some pressure on your chest with your left arm.)

Once you are familiar with the sensation of a much shorter, 'wound-up' backswing, adopt your normal grip, and recapture that same feeling as you hit some balls. With the help of these keys you will soon learn to combine a fully coiled body turn with a compact arm swing – and believe me, that's a much more consistent formula for success.

FAULT NO.22

Wrong plane – too upright or too flat

The concept of plane is one that I know causes many players concern, but we can simplify the issue if we focus on two specific points: irst, the plane of your shoulder turn, as determined by the angle of your spine at address, and second, the position of your left arm in the backswing, relative to that of your body.

Certainly there are different reasons for swinging the club off-plane. For example, picking the club up with the hands and fanning or rolling the face open are common. But to my mind, posture has the biggest influence on your ability to swing on plane. Tip over too much from the waist and the excessive spine angle you create inevitably causes you to 'tilt' your shoulders **(1)**. As a result, your left arm will be forced to rise abruptly off your chest, and your backswing will tend to be too upright, which in turn will make your downswing plane too steep. (Deep divots, lots of skied or fat shots, pulls and/or slices are fairly sure signs of an overly upright swing.)

Alternatively, an overly erect posture position can cause the shoulders to turn on too flat a plane placing the left arm very low and tucked too tightly across the chest **(2)**. The resulting flat swing plane will tend to cause a shallow, inside attack on the ball. Symptoms include hitting behind the ball, topped or thin shots, and a general loss of power.

(1) **(2)**

FIX NO.22

Get into the 'slot' at the top

The angle at which you set your spine – ie. the angle at which you bend at the hips – **is fundamental in determining the overall shape and plane of your swing; it establishes the natural axis around which the shoulders should rotate at 90 degrees**. (Bear in mind that a tall player would swing the club on a fairly upright plane; a short player on a flatter plane.) **So before you check your swing, check your posture**.

Your shoulder turn and arm swing are related up to a point. But in a good backswing the left arm should, ideally, swing on a slightly higher plane than that of the shoulders. Why? Because this allows the arms to have more of a free passage back to the ball on the downswing. Try the following test: swing to the top, and hold your position for a second **(1)**. Now slowly loosen your grip and let the shaft fall. **If the club hits you on the tip of your right shoulder, your swing is on plane (2)**. But if it hits your head or neck, you are too upright; conversely, if it falls behind you, missing your body altogether, your swing is too flat.

Either way, this drill will help to improve your action: grip a club with your left hand only, then grab your left wrist with your right hand and make a backswing **(3)**. Try to keep the upper part of your left arm in contact with your chest as you turn your shoulders, and you should sense that the club is over your right shoulder at the top. Here, it's on plane. (A mirror is a useful tool in helping you check your plane.)

(1)   **(2)**   **(3)**

CHAPTER 4
Downswing, Impact, Finish

"Characteristic of all great players is the
smooth, co-ordinated movement of the
club and the body as the downswing
begins – leading to various components
matching up through impact to allow
the essence of good shotmaking to take
place; an on-line accelerating clubhead
striking the ball and swinging through
to a balanced finish."

FAULT NO.23

'Hitting from the top'

X 'Hitting from the top' describes a downswing which features a violent change of direction, and although this is a fault which primarily dogs higher handicappers (it is probably the single biggest cause of slicing), even good players can suffer from it occasionally.

The initial move down (or transition) from the top of the backswing into the downswing establishes the rhythm and motion of the club as it returns to the ball. Problems arise when that critical change of direction is made too quickly – or aggressively – in an attempt to hit at, or kill, the ball. When you lunge forward with your upper body the club is forced to approach the ball too steeply, far outside the ideal downswing plane (often termed swinging 'over the top' – basically the major reason for golfers slicing and pulling the ball). And whatever you choose to call it, the end result is a jerky, tense-looking swing in which your head and right shoulder are overly active, resulting in a loss of both power and accuracy.

Fix No.23

Think 'swing' the clubhead, not 'hit' the ball

Characteristic of all great players is the smooth, coordinated movement of the club and the body as the downswing begins. There is no urgency to hit or kill the ball from the top. **The lower body initiates the downswing movement, and the body as a whole is then able to unwind in one synchronized motion**. This action produces a swinging motion of the arms, hands and the club which appears effortless and allows the acceleration of the clubhead to peak through impact.

To improve the fluidity of your swing as the club changes direction from backswing to downswing, try this exercise: take your 6-iron, and, with your feet only a few inches apart, hit a few shots. Swing smoothly back **(1)**, and let your lower body unwind to initiate the start of the downswing **(2)**. **Make the transition as smooth as you can; sense a 'softness' in your hands and arms, and simply let the club fall** – let gravity pull it down before releasing the clubhead through impact. (Keeping your head steady as your downswing starts will further calm your upper body, so allowing the club to approach the ball from the inside, on a much more shallow plane.) This will help you to **appreciate the sensation of swinging the clubhead through the ball as opposed to hitting at it**. After a while, graduate to your normal stance. Your swing should feel effortless, and the ball should really fly!

(1) **(2)**

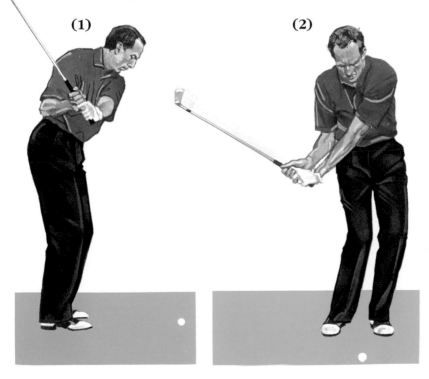

FAULT NO. 24

'Over the top' feel/club jammed behind body

X This, predominantly, is a good player's fault, and it manifests itself like this: whenever a shot goes to the left, they think they have come 'over the top'. So they over-react. They try to get the club moving into the ball more from the inside (ie. more from in-to-out). This, or so they believe, will stop them hitting the ball left.

Sadly, they're mistaken. What actually happens is that such a severe 'in-to-out' swing narrows the downswing arc to such an extent that the right arm gets 'jammed' in behind the body, where it usually remains flexed for far too long **(1)**.

From such a cramped position as this, two things are possible – either the club is not released, and the shot is blocked to the right, or, if the right arm does somehow manage to straighten at the last moment, excessive use of the hands closes the clubface through impact, sending the ball to the left **(2)**. Hence the 'over the top' feeling.

A tell-tale sign? Your divots point to the right of the target. That's the giveaway. In a true 'over the top' swing the divots point left. Which just goes to show that feelings can sometimes be misleading.

(1)

(2)

Fix No.24

Widen your downswing arc

☑ **The key here is to straighten and release your right arm as early as possible from the top of the swing**. This may feel like you are 'casting', but as long as you maintain the angle – or cock – at the back of your right wrist, you need not concern yourself. Together with the gradual opening of your upper body toward the target as your body unwinds, this will serve to widen your downswing arc, and gets the club approaching the ball on a much squarer path.

This two-part exercise will help you: **(1)** grip a short iron with your right hand only, and attempt to hit some shots off a tee. From the top of your backswing, sense the immediate straightening of your right arm. This will prove difficult at first, but work at it. You will soon begin to appreciate the benefit of greater freedom and space for your right arm, and sense the club swinging down the target line. **(2)** Take a wedge, or 9-iron, and gripping the club normally, try to re-create the same sensation that you felt in step one. Focus on making solid contact and check to see that your divots are looking squarely at – or even slightly left of – the target.

These drills will help you to appreciate the correct motion of the right arm on the downswing. **They will encourage you to get the club swinging on a path more from in-to-square-to-in (as opposed to in-to-out), keep your hands passive and allow the clubface to release squarely through impact**.

(1)   **(2)**

FAULT NO.25

Poor weight transfer / 'no legs'

It goes without saying that a good weight transfer is a prerequisite for a solid, powerful swing. Watch good ball strikers in action and you will see they shift their weight instinctively. They appreciate the importance of gathering momentum, and, such is the subtlety of the motion in their feet, knees and hips, they appear to shift their weight effortlessly.

Such fluency of movement is not something that characterizes the swing of the average amateur player. I see too many examples of a poor lower body motion where, through impact, for example, the right foot is flat on the ground, the player's weight languishes on his right side, the legs virtually static. This rigidity in the lower body destroys any hope of a good weight transfer and so greatly reduces clubhead speed, encouraging instead a weak, 'scoopy' hand action through the ball.

Fix No.25

Clang the knees for an improved leg action

✓ I get very excited when I talk about improving leg action, because I know how quickly it can benefit a player's performance. So if you've been guilty of neglecting your lower body motion for some time, here is a great drill to give you the proper understanding.

Here we go: first, address a 7-iron shot as you would normally, but lift your right heel up off the ground. Then – still keeping your right heel up – swing the club back, making sure that the majority of your weight is on your right side at the top – feel it supported on your toes **(1)**. Finally, as you swing down and through 'impact', **try to get your right knee to drive toward your left**; imagine there are cymbals attached to each, and that you are trying to clang them together as loudly as possible **(2)**.

Feel the difference? **As your right knee 'kicks in' on the downswing, your hips should clear out of the way as your left leg straightens to support the transfer of weight**. This will result in greater clubhead speed. Keeping your right heel off the ground has simply 'woken up' your feet, knees and hips; they're part of the action. Now, simply retain this 'cymbal' feeling with your regular stance, and your much improved lower body motion will enable you to shift your weight correctly onto your left side – a powerful move indeed.

(1)   **(2)**

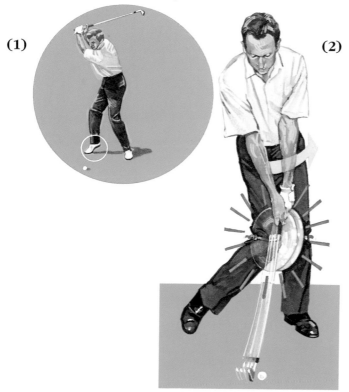

FAULT NO.26

Early release/'casting' the clubhead

If you were to compare high-speed swing sequences of good ball strikers in action, a common position that would invariably catch your eye is the remarkable way in which they retain their wrist-cock deep into the hitting area. It's the proverbial 'late-hit'; good players are able to create tremendous 'clubhead lag', storing energy until the last possible moment, before finally unleashing the clubhead through the ball.

In contrast, the majority of poor ball strikers lose this 'lag' much too early in their downswing. They suffer an 'early hit', (often referred to as 'casting' the club). As a result they sacrifice whatever power they might have stored in the backswing, and end up with a very weak, 'slappy' hit, the clubhead decelerating through impact.

Symptoms of such an early release can be classified as follows: pre-impact – loss of the angle at the back of the right wrist, the club and left arm virtually forming a straight line **(1)**; impact – a 'scoopy' position, the hands either level with, or slightly behind, the ball; post-impact – the right hand wraps over the left as the left wrist collapses **(2)**.

In fact, another clue to this fault is that you hit your woods reasonably well, but strike your iron shots poorly – ie. not solid, no divot. If that sounds familiar you can assume you are an 'early releaser'. You can get away with an early release more with a wood than an iron, because you can sweep a wood shot, but in order to really strike your iron shots crisply, your left wrist must be ahead of the clubhead through impact.

(1)

(2)

FIX NO.26

Delay your release for solid contact

✓ Before we work on improving your downswing, let me stress **you cannot just put yourself in this powerful, delayed-release position**. Remember, **it's a moment captured in a series of good movements, and so can only be achieved in conjunction with a correctly moving body**.

Try this excercise to appreciate the sensation associated with a 'late-hit'. First, take hold of a club and place your left hand below your right (ie. a cross-handed grip), making sure that at least three knuckles are visible on the back of your right hand. Then, as you make your backswing, notice how your right wrist really hinges, and then try to maintain that wrist cock for as long as you can on the downswing before releasing the clubhead through 'impact' **(1)**. When you do this correctly, it should feel as if you are leading with the butt-end of the club before finally allowing the clubhead to whip through in time for impact .

To further appreciate the sensation of impact, take your 5-iron and address a corner of a wall, or some other immovable object **(inset)**. Put your body into the impact position, then push the clubhead into the wall and feel your hands slightly ahead, **your left wrist flat** (looking at the target), **and a cupped angle formed at the back of your right wrist**. Hold this isometric position for a few seconds, then repeat the exercise. Now try to re-create these feelings of 'lag' and 'impact' when hitting some balls – you will not believe the improvement in your striking **(2)**.

(1)

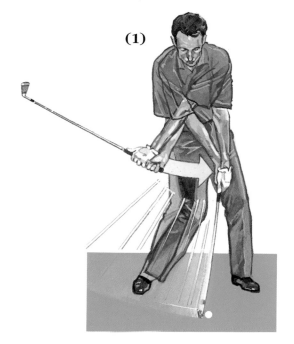

(2)

FAULT NO.27

Leg overdrive – sliding ahead/reverse 'C'

X This is a fault that I see mainly in better players, and, to a certain extent, it's a problem that stems from the well-worn adage 'drive your legs for power'.

Of course, the notion that the legs are a source of power is quite correct up to a point. But their role is much more subtle than that. They also provide stability and balance. Your legs provide the essential resistance in your swing that enables you to wind and unwind your trunk effectively. And that's where real power comes from. Used correctly, your legs facilitate the powerful rotation of your trunk, which in turn translates into a free, accelerating arm motion and great clubhead speed.

Problems arise when your legs drive too hard towards the target in the downswing. As the lower body drives, the upper body will be left too far behind the ball, placing a lot of strain on the lower back. This 'hanging back' of the upper body places the emphasis once again on the hands and arms; they must play catch-up to square the clubface in time for impact. Sometimes they will, sometimes they won't. But whether they do or not, you invariably end up in the classic reverse 'C' finish position. And that only benefits your chiropractor.

Fix No.27

Feel the benefit of a firm left side

In order to hit the ball solidly (and consistently), it is important that through impact you hit into what we describe as a **firm left side**. In other words, for the position that you achieve at impact to be effective, the left side of your body must be firm enough to both support and resist the release of the clubhead as your trunk unwinds. A weak or 'soft' left side (ie. that which we would associate with an overly flexed left leg, or one that slides too far forward) affords no resistance as there is nothing to hit against.

Although you will feel inhibited at first, turning your left foot slightly inwards when you practise will serve to eliminate any tendency that you may have to 'slide' your left side through impact, and encourage a much better rotation of your upper body against the resistance of a braced left leg through the hitting area **(1)**.

The result is a much more efficient release of the torque that you create in your backswing, which is bound to be reflected in the quality of your ball striking. **Notice, too, how much straighter your body is at the finish, and how flat your left foot is on the ground, as opposed to rolling over (2)**. As a final check, place an umbrella outside your left foot at address. Swing to the finish without knocking it over and you have obviously eliminated any 'slide'.

(1)

(2)

FAULT NO.28

Dominant left side/poor body release

X For years golfers have been told to 'pull hard with the left side; don't use your right side'. That's misleading advice. For just as golf is a two-handed game, the golf swing is essentially a two-sided affair. And it must be treated as such if you want to get the most out of it.

Any tendency to pull continuously from the top of your swing with your left side creates a whole series of complications. Most noticeably, your left arm is forced away from your body through impact, which in turn raises your left shoulder and tilts your right side down too low **(1)**. Your upper body ends up 'closed' in relation to the target line; the right side effectively 'blocked out' of the shot altogether.

The result is a swing that delivers the club to the ball too much from the inside **(2)**, leaving you no option but to employ a 'hands-orientated' release through impact in order to start the ball on line. And the problem only gets worse if your bad shot goes left. Instinctively you'll think, 'Uh-oh, too much right hand; better pull harder with the left side'. And despite what your feelings may tell you, that is wrong.

(1)

(2)

Fix No.28

Move the left, then fire the right

✓ Although both sides of your body play significant roles in your golf swing, they do so at different times. True, more emphasis should be placed on the left side as you start down. But then, at about the halfway stage, the right side of your body must take the leading role. **Assuming you are in the correct hitting position, you can fire through the ball as hard as you like with your powerful right side**. It's all a matter of timing.

Here's how to get that feeling of both sides working in harmony. With a ball positioned in the middle of your stance, draw your right foot back until the toe of your right shoe is level with the heel of your left, but keep your hips and shoulders square to your target line. Then, from the top of the backswing, you want to feel that the pulling motion of your left side and the downward motion of your left arm move in conjunction, while your right foot, knee and hip remain in place and resist for a fraction of a second. When the club then moves down to about hip height, your right side (including the right arm and hand) needs to take over through impact – go ahead and rip through the ball – just as if you were hitting a forehand tennis stroke **(1)**. **With the correct action, you should be aware of your hands and left arm being closer to your body through impact (2)**, **as your chest opens up to the target, and the club moves back to the inside**.

(1)

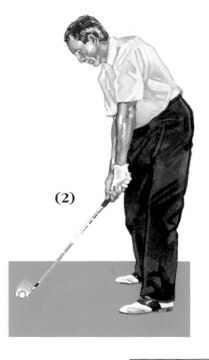

(2)

FAULT No.29

No extension past impact

It often amazes me how many players make a great looking practice swing, really zipping the clubhead through 'impact', but who then fail to reproduce that same acceleration when the ball is put in front of them. They seem inhibited; it's as if their thoughts turn to hitting at the ball, rather than swinging freely through it.

The illustration depicts a fairly common swing position for many amateurs – particularly those who slice. Lacking the confidence to accelerate the club correctly, they lose the momentum of their swing; in the absence of any flowing clubhead speed, their arms effectively 'collapse' through impact. There's no 'free-wheeling' sensation; no centrifugal force there to get the arms extended and pull them through.

Just as a sprinter would aim to accelerate through the finish tape, you as a golfer, must aim to accelerate the clubhead all the way through impact. To that end, you must learn to maintain the radius of your swing arc all the way through the hitting area.

Fix No.29

Swing the club 'baseball' style

Watch a lumberjack chopping a tree and you'll see that **his arms are fully extended** as the axe makes contact with the wood **(1)**. Experience has taught him that this is the most effective way to deliver a forceful blow. The same is true of the baseball player smashing a home run. And the same is true in golf, too.

Following this principle, it's a good idea to practise making swings on the same horizontal plane as the baseball player. With a club (a driver is fine) held out in front of your body at about waist high, try to swing it back and forth with the feeling that your arms are fully extended through the impact area. (Swinging two clubs together is another good exercise to encourage the correct release; the added weight will pull your arms through.)

Once you have that feeling of this release, gradually lower the club until you can swing it on a normal plane. **Focus on keeping that triangle formed by your arms and shoulders intact as you accelerate and extend the club through impact and on towards the finish position (2).**

(1) **(2)**

FAULT No.30

Poor follow-through position

X Almost without exception, great players finish their swing with a stylish and distinctive follow-through position; it's their trademark, if you like. And they make a habit of stamping it on every full shot they hit, much like the artist signing his name to a finished painting.

Of course, to a large extent, the quality of your follow-through position is determined by what precedes it. But it is necessary that you at least have an awareness of where you need to get to if you want to stand a chance of making a good swing.

A poor follow-through is invariably the result of an inhibited body motion, coupled with a decelerating clubhead. Such a position often stems from a player's tendency to guide – or 'steer' – the clubhead through impact, as opposed to freely releasing the club in the downswing and 'letting it all go'. This fault is typified by the player who finishes his swing with too much of his body weight on his right side, and the club stuck up in the air. Hardly an elegant way to sign off.

FIX No. 30

Make your finish picture perfect

To fully finish your swing **the right side of your body must be encouraged to rotate all the way through the shot so that you end up with the majority of your weight on your left side, your right foot up on its toes (1)**. Ideally, your knees should be gently touching, your hips fully turned, and **your right shoulder looking at the target**. (Quick check: as you complete your swing, your weight should be so finely balanced on your left foot that you could almost walk through the shot toward the target.)

Having that understanding of where your body should be will help you to achieve the ultimate follow-through pose; one the pro's make routine. Copy them. When you make a practice swing, accelerate through the shot so far that **the club almosts hits you on the back**, then **recoil it back down** to about hip-height, and **hold that pose for a second (2)**. Now you're looking good.

This recoil action will make you fully aware of how the club must accelerate and 'release' all the way to the finish. Once you feel comfortable, try it with the ball in front of you. Your swing may not be a masterpiece, but your shots should definitely improve.

(1)   **(2)**

CHAPTER 5
Common Flaws

"Successfully linking all the
components of a golf swing together is
the ultimate in building a co-ordinated,
repeating action. However, to produce
consistent shots, it requires not only
looking at the parts of a swing in
isolation, but at the complete picture
as a whole."

FAULT NO.31

Excessive head movement

X You may have noticed this fault on video, seen it in your shadow, or been made aware of it by a fellow golfer. Whatever, trying to fix excessive head movement by consciously keeping your head rigid only results in tension, anxiety and a golf game that only gets worse.

An important point to remember is that excessive head movement is generally the effect of poor body rotation, and any discussion about head movement in the golf swing must also take into account the movement of the spine. The two, after all, are attached. If the spine angle you establish at address should change appreciably during your swing, your head position will obviously move in tandem with it, resulting in compensations having to be made in order to hit the ball solidly.

Head movement can be classified in any one – or any combination – of the following ways: **(1)** from side-to-side, **(2)** up and down, and **(3)** toward and away from the ball-to-target line. In a good swing you usually see a bit of (1) and, occasionally, a little evidence of (2). A small amount of movement is, in fact, perfectly acceptable. Too much, however, can lead to fat or thin shots. Of the three, (3) is by far the most dangerous, whether that movement be forward then back, or vice versa. Either way, your weight is rocking excessively toward your toes or heels, which affects your balance, and can result in shots being struck off the toe or the heel of the club.

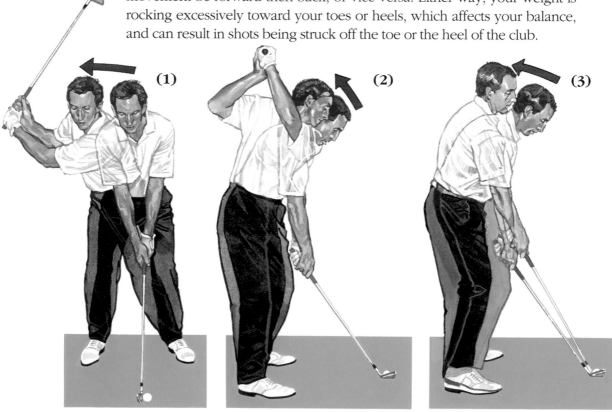

(1)   (2)   (3)

FIX No.31

Focus on your spine angle

✓ **One of the biggest keys to a repeating swing, and a fairly steady head, is to focus on maintaining the spine angle (as established at address) until just after impact**. In order to facilitate the correct rotation of your trunk, **your head must be allowed to rotate a little as well**. If your head position were to remain static, your ability to turn your body and subsequently transfer your weight would be greatly inhibited.

The following drills will help you to appreciate the desired motion. First, place a cushion between your head and a wall, then fold your arms across your chest and adopt your normal address posture. Now, keeping that cushion against the wall, work on your pivot motion. Sense that your trunk rotates around a fairly steady head, but allow your head to swivel slightly to help your rotation **(1)**. Don't worry if the cushion falls out after 'impact'. By then the ball will already have gone.

Now turn around, adopt your normal posture, but this time rest your rear-end against the wall **(2)**. Keep it fixed in place as you repeat that pivot motion back and through. Focus this time on the angle of your upper body; sense how that angle remains constant until just after 'impact'.

Given time, these drills will give you the proper feeling of the correct trunk motion during the swing, and so gradually rid you of any excessive head movement.

(1)

(2)

FAULT NO.32

Arms and body out of sync/poor timing

 In golf instruction, we often talk about the importance of 'timing'; that magical ingredient which synchronizes perfectly the fluid turning of your body with the smooth swinging of your arms, resulting in the effortless release of the clubhead through impact. Whatever your handicap, you've probably experienced that tremendous sensation when your timing was 'pure'; you're hitting the ball right out of the middle of the club, with little apparent effort. Happy days.

But, as always, there's a flip side. For some unknown reason, your timing goes awry. Your arms and body seem to be at odds; these fundamental components of your swing are 'fighting' each other, and the game quickly becomes one long, demoralizing, struggle.

There are a number of possible reasons why this discord creeps in, but problems generally begin to arise when the upper parts of your arms separate from your rotating chest at the halfway stages in your backswing and follow-through. This can be seen easily with the benefit of slow motion video playback. The left arm appears to be separating and lifting from the chest in the backswing, the right arm similarly out of position on the through-swing. Synchronizing the motion of the arms and the body through impact with this fault is, at best, unlikely.

Fix No.32

Learn to appreciate the value of 'linkage'

My hope is that by now you appreciate that **successfully linking your arm and body motion together is the ultimate in building a co-ordinated, rhythmical swing**. To that end, the sensation you must strive for is that of **the pressure being maintained between your upper arms and your chest**, at least to the halfway stages in your backswing and follow-through. The left arm should lie diagonally across your chest on the backswing; the right arm in a mirror-image position on the through-swing. The following drill will help you to achieve this **linkage**.

Tuck a head cover firmly under each armpit, and work on keeping them both in place as you make easy, three-quarter-length swings with a 9-iron. **Concentrate on rotating your body and swinging your arms in unison**; synchronize your overall movement, and pretty soon you will be striking the ball consistently. (**This exercise is designed to train no more than a three-quarter-length swing**. In a full swing the head covers would be expected to fall out as the arms rise up the chest to form a good backswing position.) Once you feel comfortable with these three-quarter swings, dispense with the head covers and try to recreate the same linked feeling as you graduate to hitting full shots. With a little practice your swing will feel effortless. Your timing will quickly return, and the game will seem easy again.

FAULT NO.33

Too quick, too slow; poor tempo

X Tempo is basically the overall speed of your swing. Put another way, it refers to the time that it takes to complete your golf swing from start to finish – somewhere in the vicinity of just over a second. When you're playing well – hitting the ball long, solid and accurately you will find that your tempo is pretty much the same with every full swing that you make. But when your game is off, your natural tempo usually goes with it. Sounds straightforward enough. But what, exactly, should your natural tempo be?

Generally, a player's tempo should reflect his personality. For example, if you're a quick-talking, fast-moving individual, your swing will tend to be fairly up-beat to match. But if, on the other hand, you're a relatively laid-back, easy-going sort of person, your swing will be similarly unhurried, easy by nature.

Whatever your natural demeanour, it's important, for a consistent tempo, that you start your swing with a co-ordinated movement of the club, arms and body together. Any tendency to over-control the club with excessive use of the hands and arms spells trouble; for whether you move it away at a snail's pace, or snatch it back too quickly, the tempo of your swing is immediately destroyed.

FIX NO.33

Relax, then think 'smooooth'

☑ **The start of your swing is the key to your overall tempo**. As the club moves away from the ball, the body should begin to turn in unison. In other words, **your hands and arms must move in synchronization with the rotation of your trunk**.

In order to achieve this you must be relaxed as you prepare to make your swing. Take a few deep breaths, and exhale fully as you waggle the club a few times **(1)**. Also, to get your swing flowing from the start, it is helpful to get yourself a swing trigger. Watch the pro's on TV, and pick up on their pre-swing habits. One that I particularly like involves nothing more complicated than kicking the right knee in slightly immediately prior to moving the club back **(2)**; a simple trigger, but it helps to get the whole motion started. Then **think 'smooooth', not slow**, as you move everything away from the ball **(3)**.

Here's another idea that will help you work on your overall tempo: address a ball, then raise the clubhead off the ground slightly, move it forward to a position about two feet into the follow-through, and start your swing from there. Glide the clubhead back over the ball, complete your backswing and swing through hitting the ball all in one continuous movement. Repeat this a number of times and gradually you will appreciate the sensation of creating good tempo. Get working on a consistent tempo and you'll see amazing results in your ball striking.

(1)

(2)

(3)

SMOOOOTH.

FAULT No. 34

Jerky swing – lack of rhythm

X Whether a swing is fast or slow, the various stages that comprise the overall motion must be blended together to form one continuous movement. Here's where we distinguish rhythm from tempo: your overall tempo may be fast, it may be slow. But if your swing is at all jerky, you won't reap the benefit of a good rhythm.

The biggest problem area as far as maintaining rhythm is concerned is the transition period between the backswing and the downswing. Why? Because too much emphasis is placed on breaking the swing down into a backswing *and* a downswing, when really it should be treated as a single, fluid motion. This is certainly aggravated by the fact that many golfers are trying to kill the ball from the top of the swing, and as a result ruin the all-important transition from back to down.

If, during a typical round, you tend to hit a lot of good shots, but mar your performance with the odd costly nightmare, it could well be that your swing technique – for the most part – is pretty good, but that your rhythm is sometimes inconsistent.

Fix No.34

Rhythm – the oil that keeps you swingin'

I like to think of the golf swing as a chain reaction; one good move leads to another. The swing can certainly be broken down into many stages, but something that takes just over a second to complete has to be thought of as a total motion. Working on positioning should, for the most part, be reserved for practice time in front of a mirror, where no ball is involved. **Rehearse the various links of the swing enough that they become habitual**; so when you do make a swing they simply form a part of a fluid motion from start to finish.

To get your rhythm working for you from the start, you need to be relaxed at address. Then work on swinging to a beat. Pace yourself when you practise – **think of your swing as a one-and-two motion**. Say the words out loud: **'one' is your backswing … 'and' signals the transition or change in direction … 'two' your motion through the ball to the finish**. 'Back-and-through', or 'turn-and-turn' work just as well. It's a simplistic approach, but using these phrases in a sing-song manner is a great way to improve your overall rhythm. Practise it by making swings with your eyes closed – feel the weight of the club and sense its speed gradually accelerating from the top of your swing all the way through to a controlled finish. Then recreate that same rhythm on the golf course and see how your consistency improves – even your bad shots will be better.

FAULT No.35

Losing your balance / poor footwork

X Have you ever noticed how great players always seem to swing in perfect balance, no matter what sort of shot they are hitting? They make it look so easy, too. Whether they are playing a three-quarter pitch or a full-blown drive, they always finish with their body in a controlled, poised position.

There's a valuable lesson here: simply, in order to accelerate and release the clubhead squarely into the ball at impact, good balance is vital. The source of that balance is the area from your hips down to your feet. Up until just before impact (where they then play an active part), the lower body should remain passive; its role is to stabilize and support the rotation of the trunk and the swinging of your arms.

Problems arise when your hips, knees and feet become overly active. If your weight should move excessively toward your heels or toes (or roll onto the outside of your ankles) your balance and stability, due to a severe shifting in your centre of gravity, will immediately be disrupted, throwing the path of your swing into disarray. And there's no telling what might happen then … .

Fix No.35

'Brace' your knees, and swing in balance

☑ Although it may feel a little awkward at first, the following drill will help you to appreciate the athletic role of the lower body, both in terms of balancing the swing and injecting a little extra 'thrust' through impact, where speed obviously matters most.

It works like this: address a ball as you would normally, but turn both feet in a few degrees, and sense the width of the gap between your knees **(1)**. **Then, as you make your swing, try to maintain that gap until just before impact (2)**, whereupon close it as quickly as you can as you **'fire' your right hip, knee and foot through towards the target (3).** The resistance that you will feel in your lower body should really help your balance, especially through the all-important impact area.

Another great way to improve your leg action is to hit full shots from a fairway bunker – but without digging your feet into the sand. I often use this exercise with tour players whenever their balance is a little off. On a delicate footing, the only way to stay in balance and make solid contact is to 'quieten' your leg action. Try it; you'll be amazed at the results.

One more thing. If you find that your left heel needs to rise off the ground for you to complete your body pivot, then let it. Some players, notably senior golfers who lack flexibility, would probably benefit from raising their left heel a little. That's understandable. But as a general rule, for better balance don't lift it unless you really have to.

(1)   **(2)**   **(3)**

Fault No. 36

Losing your swing; losing your 'feel'

X The saying 'I've got it, I had it, I lost it,' is no doubt familiar to you – I refer to it as the golfer's 'epitaph'. And it's especially applicable when it comes to describing that elusive quality every swing needs: 'feel'.

Golf is such a fickle game. Your swing may feel good one day, but be gone the next (even though you're playing with the same key thoughts). Your rhythm vanishes without a trace, the club weighs a ton, you lose distance … any number of things can suddenly – and quite inexplicably – 'go'.

If this all sounds horribly familiar, don't worry. It's a problem that befalls even the very best players. Any one of a number of things can cause it – you name it, a change in the weather, rushing onto the first tee, a bad night's sleep, playing with a long hitter … anything.

Only one thing's for sure – whatever the reason for this sudden loss of feel, all manner of bad shots result. As frustration sets in, the happy frame of mind you may have enjoyed only yesterday is a distant memory.

ONE DAY...

GREAT SHOT! —

NEXT DAY....

FORE! —

Fix No.36

Various thoughts on recapturing feel

✔ First off, don't be too hard on yourself when your 'feel' deserts you. It happens to everyone. You just have to realize that your golf swing will, to some degree, vary from day to day, week to week. That's what makes golf the great game it is. What you need is an emergency 'checklist', so that when things do start to go sour, you can quickly go about getting back on track. Here are a few ideas.

• **Start with your fundamentals**: check your grip, posture, and alignment. Any problems there will affect your swing and your feel.

• **Make the most of your past experience**: what did you work on the last time you lost your swing? Fall back on that knowledge. Check for signs of any old faults, too. Often without realizing it, old habits have a tendency to come back to haunt you.

• **Take your mind off hitting the ball**, and think more in terms of making a fluent swing. Make a few practice swings with your eyes closed. Feel the weight of the clubhead, and sense your rhythm and balance.

• **Force yourself to 'club-up' out on the course**. If you find yourself in a situation that would normally call for a 5-iron, play an easy 4-iron instead. Swing within yourself at about three-quarter pace until you start to hit the ball solidly again.

• Once you've recaptured your feel, remember to **write down your most successful swing-keys when you are playing well**. Then you can refer back to them the next time your swing is off.

FAULT NO.37

Slices and pulls

X Believe it or not, these faults stem from the same fundamental swing flaw. In each, the clubhead approaches the ball on an out-to-in swingpath; it's one of the most common faults in golf. (Quick check: if your divots consistently point to the left of the target, you're swinging from out-to-in.)

As to the outcome of the shot, the position of the clubface at impact is the deciding factor: if it's closed (or square), the ball will be pulled to the left of the target; if the face is open, the shot will be sliced away to the right with severe clockwise spin.

Generally speaking, the slicing action of an out-to-in swing is most sorely felt with the longer clubs, the low-numbered irons and woods. These straight-faced clubs are much less forgiving to this kind of swing path, and the ball spins uncontrollably to the right. Pulls often occur with short irons – the greater loft encourages backspin, which tends to negate the effects of the sidespin, so the ball goes straight to the left. Some golfers fool themselves by thinking this type of pull shot is a hook. Think again.

PULL   SLICE

Fix No.37

Square the clubface, improve the path

To eliminate pulls and slices you must not only learn to swing the club on a more in-to-out path, but also improve the position of the clubface through impact (ie. 'square it off'). You can try just one, all, or a combination of the following six pointers. It's a case of trial and error, but, believe me, the cure is in here, somewhere.

• **Strengthen your grip**. Move both hands to the right on the club until you can see three knuckles on the back of your left hand **(1)**. Make sure the 'Vs' between both thumbs and forefingers are parallel.

• **Close the overall alignment of your body** a little by aiming your feet, hips and shoulders to the right of the target. Then move the ball back in your stance.

• Close the clubface a little as you move it away from the ball; keep it 'looking' at the ball for a little longer than usual. At the top of your backswing **you should feel that the clubface is facing the sky (2)**.

• **Encourage your right arm to straighten early in the down-swing**. Imagine you were standing on a clockface, the ball bang in the centre, 12 o'clock representing the target. It should feel as if the club is swinging down from 7 o'clock through to 1 o'clock **(3)**.

• Feel the clubface closing through impact as you **encourage your right arm to aggressively cross over your left**.

• **Practise hitting shots from a sidehill lie**, with the ball positioned several inches **above** the level of your feet. This promotes a more rounded swingplane and a more powerful in-to-out path.

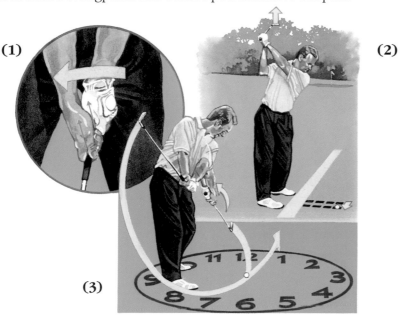

(1)

(2)

(3)

FAULT NO.38

Hooking and pushing

X In just the same way that pulled and sliced shots emanate from a similarly flawed swing, hooked and pushed shots are closely related. This time, however, the club approaches the ball on a severely in-to-out swingpath. (Quick check: your divots, in this case, will tend to look to the right of the target.)

Again, the position of the clubface at impact ultimately determines the shape of the shot that you hit. A severely in-to-out swing will result in a pushed shot to the right if the clubface is square (or slightly open) at impact; or a raking hook if the clubface is closed, imparting counter-clockwise spin onto the ball. But whatever the outcome, controlling the flight of the ball with a swing that coincides with the target line for such a brief period is all but impossible. You need to work not only on improving the position of the clubface, but on producing a swing that delivers the club on a much better line through the impact area, resulting in a straighter more accurate shot with little sidespin.

PUSH   HOOK

FIX NO.38

Clear your body, keep the clubface square

Another six-part fix: again, the best way to treat this fault is to work through each of the following points individually, and settle on the combination that works best for you. Ready?

• **Weaken your right hand grip** – ie. turn that hand to the left on the club **(1)**. That will prevent your right hand from becoming too active, and so help to keep the clubface square through impact.

• **Open up your upper body in relation to the target line at address**. Also, play the ball forward in your stance.

• **Halfway into your backswing, make sure that the toe of the club points skyward (2)**. If your problem is severe, try to feel that your left wrist is 'cupped' at the top of the swing.

• **Work on 'clearing' your body through impact**. Feel that your hips are opening up towards the target, and that your right shoulder is moving forward as you strike the ball **(3)**.

• Feel that the grip-end of the club is **swinging left after impact**, but that at the same time **the clubface remains open**.

• **Hit shots from a sidehill lie with the ball below the level of your feet.** This encourages you to swing the club on a steeper angle, thus getting it to approach the ball on a straighter line.

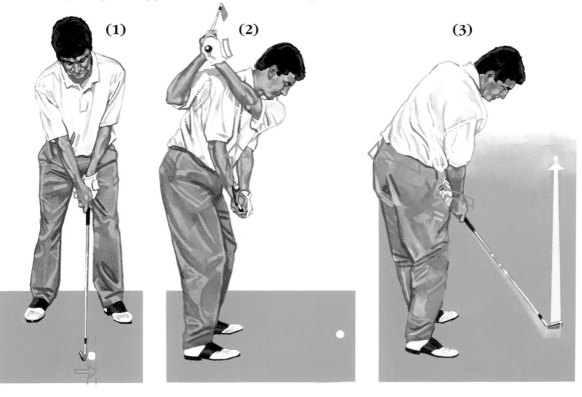

(1)   (2)   (3)

FAULT No.39

The shank

X Just hearing the 'S' word can be enough to trigger an attack of golf's most destructive shot. It's contagious, too. I've seen players start to hit the ball out of the socket just by watching others do the same. The shank, which occurs when the ball is caught in the angle between the clubface and the shaft – ie. the hosel – can result from one of two ways: either the club approaches the ball on a severe in-to-out path with the face closing, or on an equally exaggerated out-to-in path. But whichever it is, the ball disappears sideways, almost at a right angle to the intended line of flight.

In both of these cases, the basic problem is that at the moment of impact, the player's hands – and therefore the clubhead – are further away from the body than they were at address. Certainly, shanks can result from standing too close to the ball to begin with, the player thus denying the arms the room they need to swing freely past his body. But normally it is simply a case of one's weight shifting forward out towards the toes, throwing the hands and the clubhead further away from the body.

The instinctive reaction to a shank is to stand further away from the ball, thinking that will allow you to strike the ball more towards the toe-end of the club. Wrong. That actually compounds the problem, as it forces you to reach for the ball through impact, pushing even more of your weight forward onto your toes.

FIX NO.39

Weight on the heels, club on line

✓ Here's a prescription to cure the shanks. **To start with, work on a good posture and alignment. Then settle your weight back towards your heels** by curling your toes up inside your shoes. Keeping them that way throughout your swing will help to stop you from falling forward. (In severe cases, placing a golf ball under the toe of each shoe has the same effect.) **Relax your grip pressure**, too. Part of your problem is that you hold on too tight; you must allow the clubhead to swing freely and release through impact.

Next, work on improving the line of your swing through impact. Try this drill: place a ball about half-an-inch outside your object ball. Then try to hit the inner ball without dislodging the other; try **to sense that your hands are much closer to your body through impact**, and that you are going to hit the ball off the toe-end of the club. If you hit both balls, your hands and the club are still too far away from you, so you need to exaggerate the feeling even more until the sh … disappears.

Over the years I have helped a lot of players regain their confidence with these thoughts and exercises. They do work. So give them a try.

FAULT NO.40

Topped-skulled; fat-heavy shots

There's nothing worse than hitting the ball thin (no divot, ball hardly gets airborne, a big cut on the ball!) or fat (divot behind the ball, all distance lost), particularly at a crucial stage in a game. Not only do you look rather silly, but your confidence is immediately shattered; you can't help thinking that it may happen again on the next shot.

Problems such as this often occur when you try to 'lift' or 'scoop' the ball into the air, instead of allowing the loft on the clubface to do that work for you. I often see golfers fall into this trap when their lie is particularly 'tight'; to get the ball airborne they feel they have to hit 'under it'. A lack of rhythm and a failure to complete the backswing through over-anxiousness further characterize this problem. The net result is a tendency to stand up on the shot through impact and have a quick look to see where the ball has gone.

In simple terms, severe thin and fat shots are the result of an excessively steep, V-shaped swing arc. (Put another way, the clubhead isn't travelling parallel with the ground for long enough through impact.) When the bottom of the swing arc (ie. the sharp end of the 'V') falls behind the ball, the shot is hit fat; when it coincides with the top of the ball, the shot is topped.

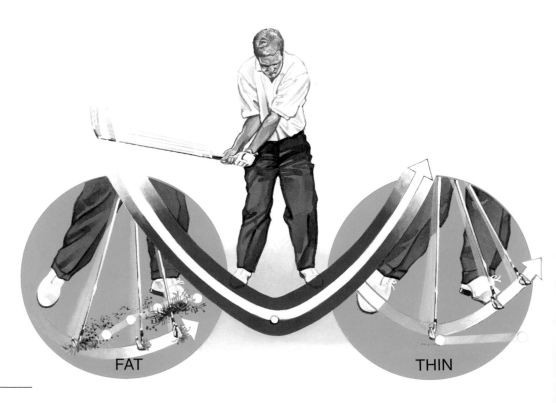

FAT

THIN

Fix No.40

Shallow the bottom of the arc

Before we look at ways in which to shallow the angle of your swing, make a note of the following important points: (1) **the ball position – forward in your stance for a wood, back for an iron** – will inevitably determine when and where on the swing arc the point of impact occurs, and (2) **the loft on the clubface will get the ball airborne** – you don't need to help it up.

There's a subtle – but important – difference between the way you strike the ball with your woods and irons. **With the wood, the clubhead sweeps the ball away with a slight ascending blow** – the clubhead making clean contact with the ball, **just past the lowest point of the arc**. To produce **the ball-turf strike that characterizes a crisply struck iron shot**, meanwhile, you need to strike the ball with a **slight descending blow** – the clubhead making contact with the ball, then the turf – **just before the lowest point of the arc**.

Now to rid your game of those undesirable shots, I want you to visualize a 'U'-shaped swing arc; one with a pronounced wide 'flat-spot' through the impact area. With a mid-iron, aim to take a shallow divot just ahead of where you ground the club; with a wood, place a tee opposite the inside of your left heel and try to clip it out of the ground without any turf contact. That will promote the sweeping action your longer shots require. With these keys in mind, I want you to **focus on completing your backswing** and then **feel on coming through your right shoulder extending forward under and past your chin**. This should help you stay down on your shots through impact and strike the ball solidly.

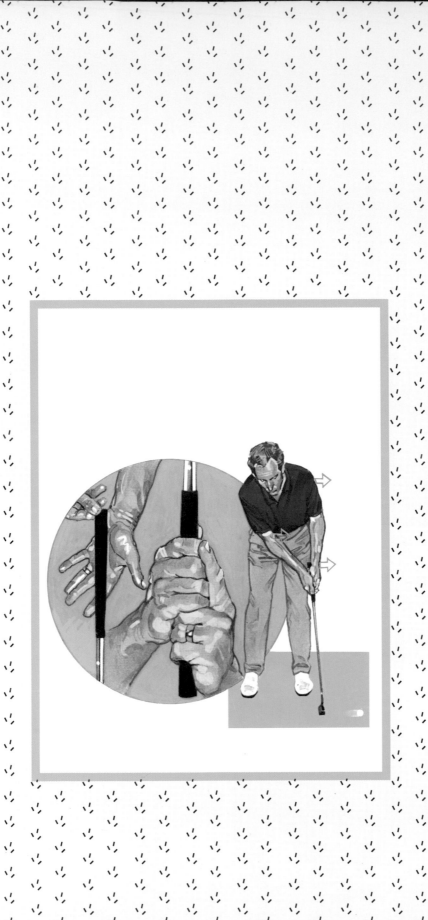

CHAPTER 6
Putting

"To think in terms of your longest, straightest tee shot counting exactly the same as a six-inch putt, puts into perspective the importance of putting. By its very nature, putting is a hugely personal matter. But whatever style you choose to trust on the greens, I believe it's important that you develop the ability to repeat a stroke which produces overspin; one which generates a consistent roll on the ball and one that combines the art of touch with the application of mechanics."

FAULT NO.41

Poor putting – faulty set-up

By its very nature, putting is a hugely personal matter. But whatever style you choose to trust on the greens, I believe it's important that you develop the ability to repeat a stroke which produces overspin; one which guarantees a consistent roll on the ball. Naturally, the quality of your address position has a direct bearing on your ability to achieve this. The way you set up dictates how easily your arms and upper body are able to work together, which in turn determines the path of your stroke and the position of the putter-face at impact.

There are two common faults that I see. First, there's the example of the player who stands very tall at address, with his legs stiff, his arms straight and his eyes outside the ball-to-target line **(1)**. Then there's the player who does just the opposite; he tends to sit down too much, his elbows are usually very bent, and his eyes too far inside the ball-to-target line **(2)**. Neither of these positions does much to encourage a uniform stroke. The arms and hands tend to work independently, rather than as a single unit in tandem with the chest and shoulders.

(1)   **(2)**

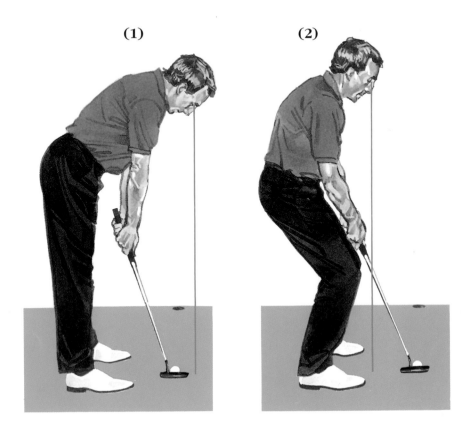

102

Fix No.41

Get set for a rock-steady stroke

I believe that the shoulder-controlled, pendulum-type stroke is the most effective for consistent putting. But for this method to work, your posture must allow your arms complete freedom of movement.

Let's build it from the ground up. In front of a mirror, take a comfortably wide stance, and flex your knees a little, as if you were just about to sit down. **Feel that your weight favours your left side a touch**, and keep your elbows relaxed and spread to the point where **your upper arms rest lightly on your rib cage (1). Your eyes should be directly over – or very slightly inside – the ball-to-target line; the ball itself should be opposite your left eye**. (Quick check: test yourself by dropping a ball from your left eye, and noting where it lands.)

Next, your alignment. Following the example that we set in the full swing, **aim the putter-face squarely to your target line, and then try to align your body parts – ie. your feet, knees, hips, forearms, shoulders and eyes – parallel to it (2)**. As long as you stay relaxed, your hands comfortably positioned either in line with, or slightly ahead of the ball (and directly beneath your shoulders), you are now in the perfect position to make a smooth stroke in which **your hands, arms and shoulders work together**.

(1) **(2)**

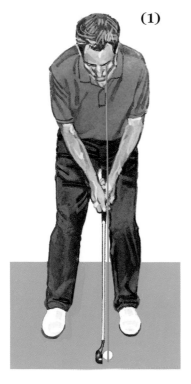

FAULT No.42

Putting – excessive body motion

X Holing putts on a regular basis is all about having the putter-face square to the intended line at the moment it contacts the ball. To do this, most good putters predominantly use a pendulum-like, arm-and-shoulder action, in which the triangle that is formed between the arms and shoulders at address can be seen to remain intact as it moves past a steady head. In other words, there is little wasted motion.

Putting problems arise when you try to 'help' the ball into the hole. When that happens, your head and upper body tend to move out of position through impact, which inevitably disrupts the alignment of the putter-face. The result is an inconsistent strike on the ball, and little or no control over the direction or the pace of the putt.

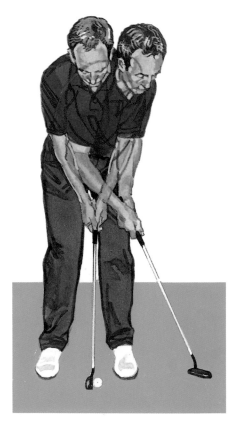

FIX NO.42

Rock your shoulders to control your stroke

✓ In putting, the fewer moving parts there are, the simpler and more consistent your method will probably be. To that end, **I encourage you to work on building a stroke that is controlled by the shoulders**.

To promote this pendulum-type action, try the following exercise. Take your address position, and place your palms together in a downward praying position. Focus on the triangle that is formed between your hands, arms and shoulders, and then, keeping your head and lower body perfectly still, **rock your shoulders so that you move the triangle smoothly back and through (1)**. Create an under-and-up pendulum motion with your shoulders, where your chest stays square to the target line, as opposed to opening your body to the hole. **Feel that your left shoulder works down on the backswing, then up on the throughswing**. This will control the path of the putter-head and keep the putter on line through impact **(2)**.

On the follow-through – particularly on the longer putts – allow your head to rotate down the line towards the target after you have completed your stroke. That enables your triangle to work correctly, and thus allows you to follow the progress of the ball all the way to the hole without lifting your body out of position.

(1)   **(2)**

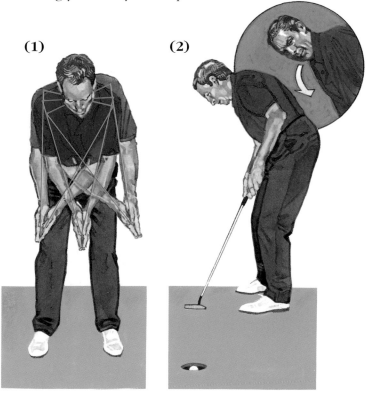

FAULT No.43

Putting – breakdown of the left wrist

X Nothing ruins the consistency of a putting stroke like unwanted wrist action through impact. This breakdown can often be seen to occur in conjunction with a shoulder motion that has either stopped or is decelerating, and is one of the most common causes of a poorly struck short or medium length putt – and this applies equally to the pro's.

With this fault, judging the pace and controlling the direction of your putts can prove to be a real problem. Because of the uncertainty that surrounds this type of wrist action in terms of the strike you impart on the ball, rarely will you release the putter with any confidence. You end up decelerating the putter through impact, which makes it virtually impossible to put a good roll on the ball.

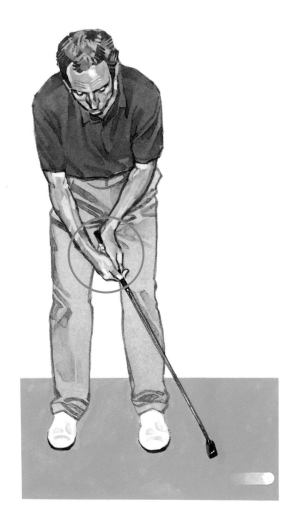

Fix No.43

'Pull' and 'push'

To help protect yourself against any unwanted hingeing in the left wrist, hold the putter so that the shaft runs high across the palm of your left hand, resting against the fleshy pad below the thumb. Then close your hand, draping your left index finger over the fingers of your right hand. Doing this forms what's known as the 'reverse-overlap' grip; **the left hand is now effectively locked in place on the club**.

Now let's put your grip to the test. Remember, in a solid pendulum stroke, the shoulders control the motion from start to finish while the hands remain passive. Try this drill: address a straight three-foot putt, and without a backswing, 'brush' the ball towards the hole. **Make the follow-through by 'pulling' with your left arm and left shoulder and 'pushing' with your right arm and right shoulder. Focus on keeping your left hand firm as you accelerate the putter past your left foot, and check to see that the putter-face is looking directly at the hole on the finish**. Repeating this drill regularly will give you the correct feel, eliminates the 'wristiness' in your stroke, and should get those putts dropping.

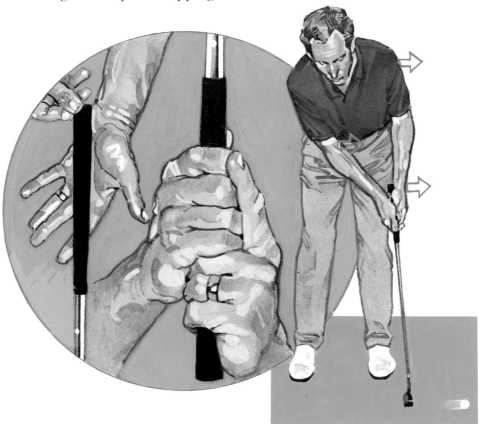

FAULT NO.44

Putting – poor distance control

X Think back to the last time you three-putted. What let you down? Your accuracy, or your inability to stroke the ball the desired distance? I'm prepared to wager that nine times out of ten, it's the latter.

On any putt over, say, ten feet, getting the distance right is much more important than direction. Even a beginner can hit a putt reasonably close to the right line, but the chances of him rolling the ball the right distance are slim. Without the experience of 'feel', he's much more likely to rap the putt miles past, or leave the ball woefully short of the hole.

To a much lesser extent, the same is true of more advanced players. Many golfers have a tendency to hit a putt 'hard' or 'soft', depending on its length. That's asking for trouble. The 'hard' and 'soft' approach is too difficult to judge; you'll never develop a consistent feel for distance. And without that, you'll always be leaving your first putt too far from the hole to be sure of getting the next one in.

Fix No.44

Longer putt, longer stroke

One of the golden rules in putting is that **the length of your stroke should always control the distance you hit the ball**. A relatively long putt requires a relatively long stroke, and vice versa. But there's a clause that you must adhere to: **no matter what the length of the putt, your tempo** – that is, the time it takes to complete your stroke – **should remain constant**. Thus, the pace of your stroke on a short putt will appear appreciably slower than that on a longer putt.

Good putters who seem to regularly hit their putts the proper distance have great tempo. With this in mind, practise putting to random targets to increase your awareness for the length of your stroke. Place tees in the green at distances of ten, 20 and 30 feet from your ball, and hit putts to all three, varying the length of your backswing for each, and making your follow-through at least as long – if not longer – than your backswing.

Always try to hit a putt firmly enough that, should it miss, the ball will finish about 18 inches past the hole. That's the optimum speed for the ball to hold its line, yet still fall in if it catches any part of the cup.

Finally, be aware that you must take into account the condition of the green and the nature of your putt – ie. uphill or downhill – when determining speed.

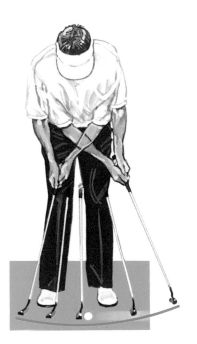
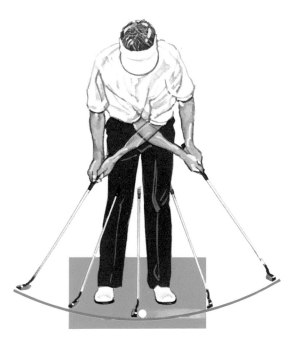

FAULT NO.45

Poor long putting

Whenever I see an amateur player sizing up a lengthy putt, or one that features several awkward slopes and borrows, my immediate reaction is to think that he or she has a very good chance of three-putting. Why? Because amateur players hardly ever practise these putts, and as a result, have poor feel. They tend to hit at the putt as opposed to stroking it.

Great putters not only hole out regularly from within six feet of the hole – that vital scoring distance – but they also have great touch and feel for distance on long putts. They realize that their goal from, say, 30 or 40 feet is simply to 'lag' the ball close enough to the hole to have a resonably simple second putt. If it goes in, that's a bonus. Keeping those three putts off the card is a must.

Fix No.45

Improve your touch

There are several things you can do to become a good lag putter mentally and physically. (1) On facing a putt upwards of, say, 40 feet, make the most of positive mental imagery – not only the line of the putt but also by **visualizing a bigger final target**. Imagine a circle with about a two-foot radius painted around the hole, and simply try to roll your approach putt within that circle. If you do, the longest putt you can have left will be two feet. (2) Be conscious that pure technique here on these lengthy putts is not a prerequisite for feel. Stand a little taller at address and **encourage a long, free stroke back and through**, and allow a little wrist action to help with acceleration. Your left wrist should, in fact, be a little cupped at the completion of the stroke.

(3) Practise long putts with your right hand only. This will give you the feeling of releasing the putter head. (4) Hit putts from one side of the practice green to the other, aiming to get each ball as close to the fringe as you can without ever going off the edge. (5) When confronted with a long lag putt on the course, take plenty of practice strokes to sense the stroke needed to execute the putt at hand.With these keys, you could surprise your friends with your new found touch on long putts.

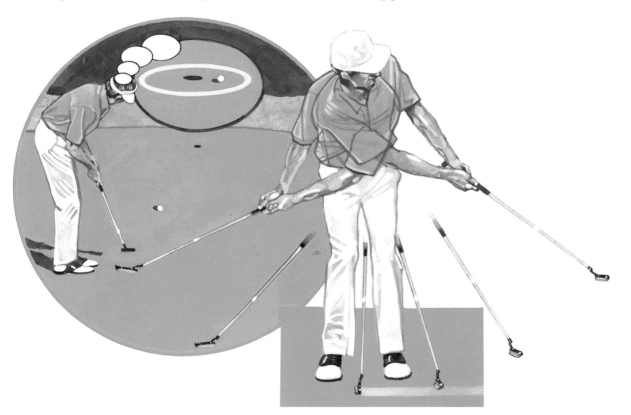

FAULT NO.46

The yips

X When you see a golfer stand and freeze over short putts, and then make an uncontrollable flinch with the putter – the ball then missing the hole, sometimes by a wide margin – you are watching someone with that nasty golfing disease the 'yips'.

Yips have been known to make people give up the game in pure frustration at not being able to accomplish something so seemingly simple as to roll a ball a short distance into a hole. The problem is basically a mental one, which, in all probability, started off as being physical. The story goes something like this: a faulty stroke results in some missed short putts. After a while, that becomes a habit; a negative image builds up in one's mind; you cannot see yourself holing a putt; you become tense and anxious; your nerves become uncontrollable and a little voice inside you says, "you are a lousy putter, you can't putt". Bingo! You have the yips.

The fault manifests itself mentally in the short putts first, because on longer putts your expectation level is lower, but, it has been known to spread. So, what can you do about the yips?

Fix No.46

Relax, holing short putts is simple

Let's tackle the mental aspect first. **All negative, self-deprecating 'inner-chatter' has to stop**. Think positively and logically. Every time you stand over a putt, **only two possible outcomes exist: you can either knock the putt in, or you can miss it**. So, accept the challenge. Make a good stroke, hit the putt solidly – if you have read it right, and the ball doesn't hit a spike mark, then it has a good chance of going in.

Okay. So now that you are in a better frame of mind, what of the physical aspects? First, you obviously need to relax. Choke down a little on the putter **and grip lightly. Keep your stroke short, accelerate through impact and listen for the ball going into the cup**. Many short putts are missed because of peeking. Practise on three-foot putts by placing a small coin under the ball and notice, say, the date. Then, strike the ball at the hole, and keep your eyes focused on the coin. **Don't look up until you hear the sound of the ball dropping into the cup**. Also, knock in some short putts with your eyes closed. This will get you **feeling your stroke instead of worrying about the hole**.

For your routine, try this: look at the hole, look back at the ball, then stroke the putt – it's that simple. **Don't wait or freeze over the ball. The less time there is to think … the better**. To build up your confidence, place six balls around the hole – about three feet away. Once you knock them all in, move to four feet. If you miss one, start over again. Get accustomed to knocking into the back of the cup. Putting is basically all confidence – get some and the word 'yips' will stand for "**Y**es, **I**'m **P**utting **S**uper"!

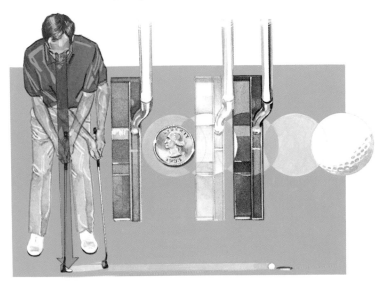

FAULT NO.47

Missing breaking putts on the low side

X Putting would be a very mundane business if each and every green was flat. Subtle slopes and borrows add spice to the game, and test the skill of the player to read the greens correctly. During the course of a typical round you are probably going to encounter many breaking putts where, in order to make the putt, you have to aim somewhere outside the hole.

In my experience, the majority of these putts are missed on the low – or 'amateur' – side, as the player fails to make enough provision for the borrow or break. In other words, more curling right-to-left putts are missed on the left side of the hole than the right, and vice versa.

The reason? Golfers often lack the confidence to start the ball outside the hole. Instinct tells you to aim at the hole, even when you know there's a definite 'break' to negotiate. As a result, from the moment the ball leaves the putter-face, the chances of the putt going in – for many players – are nil.

FIX NO.47

Focus on an intermediate target

Bearing in mind that the line and pace of every putt are inversely related, **visualize the ball running towards the hole, and try to pick out the point at which you think it will first start to break toward the cup. Regard that apex point as your intermediate target, and aim at it**. (Remember, when you read a putt, the centre of the cup may change. If your putt is breaking from left-to-right, for example, the centre could move from six o'clock to, say, eight o'clock as you look at the hole.)

Now, having chosen your line, all you have to worry about is the pace to get the ball to the hole. If you hit the ball too hard you will hit the putt right through the break; hit it too softly and even though you may have aimed correctly, it will still miss on the low side.

In the end, it all boils down to **trust. You have to trust yourself to read the break correctly, judge the speed, and then hit the putt on the line you have chosen**. If you can focus on hitting the putt to the apex of the curve, and your speed is decent, you'll have more chance of making those curly putts. Or at least start missing them on the high – or 'pro' – side.

FAULT NO.48

Lacklustre 'feel' on the greens

X There are times when putting seems so easy. You're relaxed over the ball, and the hole looks as big as a bucket. Your stroke feels perfectly grooved, the ball rolls sweetly off the putter-face, and putts disappear from everywhere. This condition is somewhat rare, I know, but it does happen.

Unfortunately, there are other times when just the opposite is true. You are tense and fidgety, and there doesn't seem to be a hole on the green. You feel generally uncomfortable, and your putting stroke is off. The ball seems to clunk off the putter, and it never appears to get up to the hole. Or, if it does, the putt lips out. You've lost your feel; the magic is gone. So what can you do about this lacklustre feel?

FIX No.48

Thoughts on recapturing 'feel'

If you sense that your feel has deserted you, work on these keys:

• **Check your alignment**. Lay a club on the ground pointing directly at a hole, and rest your putter-head on top of the shaft. Take aim, making sure the face is square (ie. that it forms a right angle with the shaft).

• **Hover the putter-head above the shaft and check the path of your stroke**. Many poorly-hit putts are the result of cutting across the line of the putt, thus producing a poor roll. In a good stroke, the putter should move slightly inside the shaft going back, then return straight through 'impact', and on towards the target.

• **Work on your rhythm. Grip lightly** to reduce any tension in your hands and arms, and learn to swing the putter freely. **Count 'one-two'** as you make your stroke – 'one' going back, 'two' coming through. That will help to enhance your tempo. If you feel you may be guilty of watching the putter-head as you move it back, hit a few putts whilst actually looking at the hole.

• **Check your routine**, too. Make, say, two practice strokes, take a couple of looks at the hole, and then stroke the putt. Develop a series of good habits, and stick to them. And remember, whatever your routine, the time you take to prepare to hit each putt should be consistent.

• **Practise putting to a tee** – that immediately takes away the pressure of 'holing it', so you can work on making solid contact. The added bonus is that out on the course, the hole appears enormous.

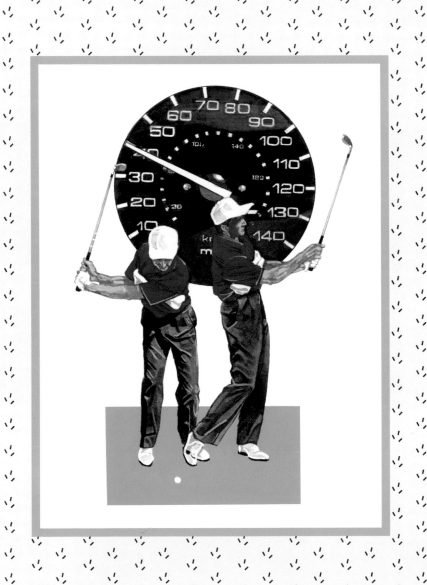

CHAPTER 7
Chipping and Pitching

"You don't need me to tell you
how important chipping is when it
comes to saving shots. Getting up and
down three or four times in a round
can turn a mediocre score into a good
score; a good round into a great round.
Versatility – both in your method and
in your thinking – is the key."

FAULT NO.49

Chipping – poor address position

X I'm sure that I don't have to tell you how important chipping is when it comes to saving shots. Getting up and down three or four times in a round can turn a mediocre score into a good score; a good round into a great round.

The key to chipping close to the hole on a regular basis is controlling the speed at which the ball rolls after it lands on the green. Only a repetitive method and practice can teach you the relationship between your stroke and the behaviour of the ball. But for your method to be effective, it must originate from a solid set-up position.

Judging the pace at which the ball 'releases' upon landing on the green is all but impossible if you play from a faulty set-up. For example, if you set up with too much weight on your right foot and the ball too far forward in your stance **(1)**; or tend to stand straight-legged and reach for the ball **(2)** – two of the most common faults that I see – the chances of making consistent club-ball contact are slim, to say the least. The clubhead is destined to approach the ball on a poor, 'scoopy' angle, which inevitably results in a mishit shot.

(1)   **(2)**

Fix No.49

Ball back, weight forward, hands forward

☑ To produce a stroke that you can repeat over and over again, adjust your set-up as follows. Firstly, **take a narrow, open stance** (ie. align your body left of the target), **position the ball back toward your right foot**, and **place a good percentage of your weight on your left side (1, 2)**. **Now push your hands ahead of the ball and feel that your chest-bone is leaning to the left of the ball**; if you like, feel that you assimilate your impact position at address. At first, you'll probably feel as if you're off balance. But persevere.

What this set-up will enable you to do is swing the club up a little on the backswing and then take a shallow divot as you return the clubhead to the ball on a downward angle. So it promotes a slightly descending angle of attack through impact – ideal for 'pinching' the ball off the turf (especially if you have a tight lie).

This exercise will help you check if you have achieved your set-up goal. Lay a shaft on the ground just outside your right foot (so that it forms a right angle with your ball-to-target line), and then make your chipping stroke **(3)**. If you have set up correctly, the clubhead should pass over the shaft both on the way back and on the way down, creating consistent ball-turf contact. Upon landing, your shots will now roll in a consistent manner each time, so making club selection much easier.

(1)   **(2)**

(3)

FAULT No.50

Chipping – stroke too 'wristy'

X Once you can appreciate how to set up to the ball correctly, you must work on making your chipping action as simple as possible. Roughly translated, that means eliminating unnecessary and unwanted wrist-action in order to produce a stroke you can trust.

Poor chipping can invariably be put down to a 'flippy' type of hand action, where the back of the left hand and wrist can be seen to collapse through impact. This occurs normally as the result of trying to help the ball up into the air, as opposed to allowing the loft of the clubface to do that for you. As a consequence, the backswing gets too long, the clubhead decelerates as the left wrist breaks down through impact and the ball is either thinned, topped or hit fat. Whatever the outcome, this relatively simple shot, that at times only has to travel a few feet, is normally botched.

FIX NO.50

Keep your wrists firm

✓ Before we look at the nature of the stroke itself, there's an important adjustment that must first be made to your grip – **strengthen your left hand** (ie. turn your left hand slightly to the right of its normal position on the grip, showing about three knuckles on the back of your hand). This will help to prevent the left wrist from breaking down through impact, which in turn will enable you to more easily control the nature of the strike you impart on the ball.

Now the stroke. **Keeping your weight on your left side**, **move the club back a short distance with a small turn of your body, keeping your wrists relaxed**, **but passive**. Then, on moving forward, **smoothly ease your knees laterally towards the target** in harmony with the **slight turning motion of your body** as you swing the club through impact. **The back of your left wrist must remain firm** as you accelerate the clubhead into the ball, and **the angle at the back of your right wrist should remain constant** throughout the entire motion. Your **follow-through must be relatively short** to ensure a crisp strike.

Test yourself to see if your wrists have stayed firm during the shot. Move your follow-through position wholesale back to your address position. Are your hands and the clubface in relatively the same position as they were when you started? If so, your wrist action is correct.

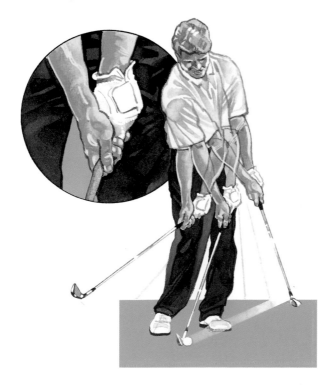

FAULT No.51

Chipping – no 'touch', no imagination

X If you are one of those golfers who seem to strike your chip shots fairly well, but rarely get the ball close to the hole, then the problem isn't necessarily in your method. It could be that your strategy around the green is letting you down.

Certainly, there's a lot more to honing a sharp short game than simply working on a good technique. To be fully versatile, you must also develop the ability to visualize and manufacture a whole array of different shots. One of the reasons why many players struggle to get up-and-down consistently is that they lack this imagination, often reaching for their favourite 'chipping club' long before they have even examined the lie of the ball or the nature of the shot they have to play.

True, it is possible to develop a good touch around the greens using only one club, but doing so calls for an exceptional amount of 'feel' and requires lots of practice. Unless you are able to invest that time and effort, I suggest that you develop a chipping system that involves learning one basic swing, and then simply vary the club that you use to play chips of differing length.

FIX NO.51

Simplify your strategy

✓ **The most effective chipping strategy is that which seeks to get the ball on the putting surface and rolling as soon as possible.** Naturally, the situation you are in must determine the ideal combination of flight and roll that you need to get the ball close to the pin, but **as a general guideline you should always aim to land the ball within ten feet of the fringe**. **Visualize the shot in your mind**; remember, the more run you need, the less lofted the club you should take, and vice versa.

Try the following test. Starting with a 9-iron, and adopting the procedure as described in Fixes Nos. 49 and 50, hit a few shots, and **concentrate on swinging the club with the same tempo every time**. Note the reaction of each ball as it rolls across the green. If your swing is repeating, they should all finish fairly close together.

Using the same strategy, now hit different clubs ranging from a 5-iron to a sand-wedge, and note the reaction of these shots. With practice, you will have a good idea of which club produces what roll. With this knowledge, you will then be able to select the correct club and hit different length chips close to the hole on the course.

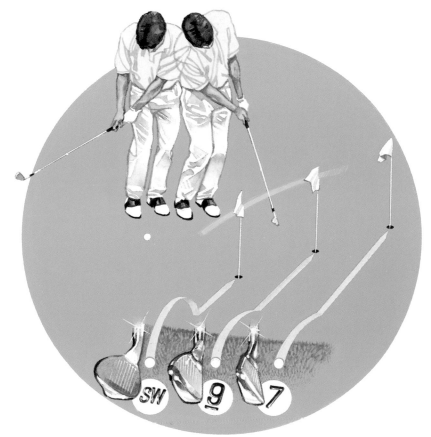

FAULT NO.52

Chipping – no confidence

X If you have ever suffered prolonged attacks of anxiety, or periods of little or no confidence in your ability to play short chip shots around the green, then you'll know only too well what an utterly soul-destroying experience it can be. The inability to execute what is, in reality, a relatively easy shot shakes the foundation of your whole game. The terms 'chilli-dip', 'fluff', 'skulled' and 'bladed' describing poorly executed chip shots come to mind, and as your nerves become increasingly ragged you begin to doubt your ability to ever get the ball close to the hole.

Such is the power of the mind. A confident player with a good short game works purely on feel and visualization – and all he sees is success. One with a poor short-game thinks only in negative terms; he gets tense and in severe cases 'freezes' over the shot. All of which shifts the golfer's focus from the 'where' to the 'how' aspect of whatever he is trying to do.

So if you are a player whose preferred choice of club is a putter on almost every occasion around the green, the following simple chipping technique should help you.

Fix No.52

Chip as you putt

The quickest way of gaining confidence in your chipping is to simplify both your thinking and your technique. One way to do that is to **regard your chipping stroke merely as an extension of your putting stroke**. Try this: with an 8-iron in your hands, set up to a ball as if you were preparing to hit a long putt. **Take your normal putting grip but play the ball back in your stance**, off the inside of your right foot. At the same time **keep your hands and weight forward, favouring your left side**, and **spread your elbows**. The club should be held almost vertically so that **the heel is raised off the ground – thus you must stand very close to the ball**. Addressing the ball in this manner positions the ball off the toe-end of the club, which, when contact is made, helps to 'deaden' and control the roll of the chip.

Controlling the stroke with a gentle rocking of your shoulders, allow the club to rise up several inches off the ground in the backswing, and then hit down on the ball slightly, clipping it into the air. **Concentrate on maintaining the width of the gap between your elbows as you swing back and through** – that ensures a pure arms and shoulders motion.

The real beauty of this method is that you take your wrists out of the equation altogether. As long as you keep your head still and focus on making a short, firm follow-through, you'll succeed in striking the ball solidly. As with putts, lengthen your stroke to play longer chips. For the very long chip shots, try experimenting with a 5- or 6-iron to get the required roll.

FAULT NO.53

Pitching – poor set-up

X I define a pitch shot as one of 60 yards or less that travels further through the air than it rolls on the ground. A standard pitch shot is normally played with a wedge or a sand-wedge – the ball is lofted reasonably high up into the air, and depending on the surface of the green, will then roll a few feet upon landing. As always, it is the way that you set up to the ball that determines the shape and consistency of the swing you are able to make.

The majority of the problems that I see players struggle with stem from the fact that they tend to set up to a pitch in exactly the same way they would to make a full swing. They align their body parallel with the ball-to-target line; for a pitch shot your lower body should be set slightly 'open' in relation to that line.

If you should mistakingly set up square to the target, the chances of you being consistent, both in terms of distance and direction, are slim. Because of the short-length swing that characterizes a normal pitch, you won't have time to square the clubface with the rotation of your body. Instead, to get the ball started on line, you are forced to manipulate the clubhead with your hands.

FIX NO.53

Pre-set the perfect impact position

In order to strike your pitch shots solidly, certain criteria must be met at impact. Specifically, your lower body should be open in relation to the target line, while your hands should be ahead of the ball.

The best way that I know to ensuring that these conditions are met on a regular basis is to pre-set them at address. Accordingly, **take a fairly narrow stance**, **and set your lower body a little open** (aligned left) to the target line. (Your shoulders and the clubface, meanwhile, should be square.) **Position the ball just forward of middle in your feet, so that your hands lie comfortably ahead**. Finally, **settle approximately 60 per cent of your weight on your left side, flex your knees and push them gently toward the target**.

This set-up is essentially the position that you want to achieve at impact. Rehearse it in front of a mirror; get used to the feeling of 'impact'. Taking it from here you can then swing confidently and hit quality pitch shots.

FAULT NO.54

Pitching – poor plane = poor shots

X With your pitch shots, your objective is to achieve pinpoint accuracy. That's why swinging the club on the correct plane is so important from short range. So small is your margin for error on this short swing, that the only way you can guarantee making good contact is to swing the club down into the ball on the correct path and angle. For a pitch, that angle will tend to be fairly steep. After all, you're using one of the most upright clubs in the bag.

Unfortunately, I see a lot of players who fail to appreciate this. A common error is taking the clubhead back severely inside and around the body, then repeating that motion through the ball and on into the follow-through. The result of this poor path and plane is that the clubhead is on line for only a very short time – if at all – drastically reducing the chances of (a) solid contact being made, and (b) the shot being on line.

Fix No.54

Club on line for solid pitches

☑ Once you are comfortable with the set-up described in Fix No. 53, work on making your swing plane more upright. As you turn and move the club away from the ball, **allow your wrists to hinge up** (don't just simply lift your arms). Sense that the shaft moves fairly vertically, both on the way back and on the way through.

With practice, you should feel that the club is much more on line approaching impact as your body turns through the shot. Work on achieving a solid ball-turf contact, and **aim to make your follow-through a virtual mirror-image of your backswing position. Think about a smooth rhythm**, too. That's important on pitch shots.

To ensure you get your pitch swing on the right plane, try this drill. Set up for a normal pitch shot then stick an umbrella (or an old shaft) in the ground about two feet outside your right foot, in line with your right heel **(1)**. Place another one the same distance outside your left foot, again keeping it in line with your heel. Then swing the club without touching either of the two umbrellas **(2, 3)**. As you swing back, hinge your wrists and try to set the club on its end so that the grip points down towards the ground. Do the same in the follow-through.

Once you have the knack of this, hit a few shots. Don't concern yourself with a particular target initially, simply work on hitting the ball solidly. Pretty soon you'll notice a big difference in the quality of your strike, and you can then focus on direction and distance.

(1) **(2)** **(3)**

FAULT NO.55

Pitching – inconsistent distance control

X It's impossible to overstate the importance of pitching in terms of the scoring equation. Good pitchers of the ball will make more birdies on short par-4's and par-5's, and usually save their par when their long approach play lets them down.

But even good players can, on occasion, find these mini-shots troublesome. Whenever a situation calls for anything less than a full swing, judging distance is an obvious problem. While it's difficult to be too far out with your direction from, say, 50 or 60 yards, it is always possible to hit the ball too far, or leave it short.

The most common cause of poor distance control can be traced to the arms and body moving independently of one another. Generally speaking, the tendency is for the swing to be either (a) too long, in which case the club tends to decelerate through impact, or (b) too short, and the clubhead is jerked through. Either way, such poor technique will inevitably cost a player many expensive strokes.

FIX NO.55

Work on the body-controlled method

✓ By now you ought to appreciate that the essence of my teaching method is that **your body controls the motion of the club** (or, as I term it, **the dog wags the tail**). I introduced you to that concept in Part 1 – The Full Swing, and the same applies here in the short game. The turning motion of your body is responsible for the way in which you release the club through impact; **increasing or decreasing the rotational speed of your trunk is the key to varying the distance of these precision shots**.

To get a feel for this, practise short pitches with a towel tucked between your upper arms and chest. Adopt the proper set up, choke down on the grip for extra control and make compact swings, keeping the towel firmly in place. Vary the speed of your body turn, and see how that affects the distance you hit the ball. **Think, on a 20-yard shot, of moving your body at 20 mph back and through; 30 yards needing 30 mph, and so on**. As you do this, keep your weight mainly on your left foot throughout the swing. Although you want to encourage body rotation, there is no need to introduce unnecessary wasted motion in the form of a significant weight transfer.

Remember, **the longer the shot, the faster you must move your body** – the added momentum you generate will naturally increase the length of your swing and the amount of clubhead speed. Constantly vary the length of your shots when you practise, so that you instinctively learn how fast to move your body in order to hit the ball the desired distance.

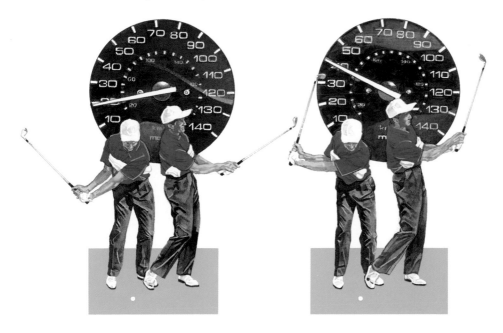

FAULT NO.56

High, soft shot – no way!

The high floating, softly landing pitch is a useful shot for any golfer to have in his repertoire – it's ideal when you have to stop the ball quickly, over a bunker to a pin cut close to the edge of the green, for example. Naturally, it's a shot that requires a great deal of touch, not to mention a certain amount of practice.

Of course, the key to executing this shot properly lies in understanding the correct technique involved. Sure, it's a tough shot to take on, but I see many golfers who make it all the more difficult by nervously trying to lift the ball up into the air. They don't appear to have much faith in the loft on the clubface doing that job for them – even though they would be using the most lofted club in their bag. Typically, save the occasional fluke, the results range from dumping the ball short into the bunker to blading it right over the green.

Fix No.56

Learning the lob

✓ **The lob should be played only when you have a reasonable lie** – ie. the ball should have a cushion of grass beneath it so that you can slide the leading edge of a sand-wedge beneath it, clipping the grass and the ball almost simultaneously. From a tight, firm lie, you should consider the risks, and probably think in terms of hitting a regular pitch shot and having to hole a reasonable-length putt to get down in two shots.

For the lob shot, **stand with your lower and upper body open in relation to the target** (for regular pitch shots only the lower body is open). **Aim the clubface to the right** (ie. lay it open), **position the ball forward in your stance**, keep your weight evenly distributed and aim to make contact with the turf a fraction behind the ball. **Focus on making a fairly lengthy, slow swing, sensing that your arms control the motion. Your hands should feel 'dead'** as the clubhead strikes the turf then the ball – **keep the clubhead swinging through to a high finish**. Obviously, standing open, you will swing the club on an out-to-in path, but with the clubface being aimed to the right, the shot will, in fact, fly straight.

Once you learn to play the lob correctly, you will see that the ball climbs steeply and lands softly, with little roll. The key is to **trust a long, slowish swing** – keep the hands quiet, and resist any urge to try and help the ball up into the air. Oh, **and to practise!**

FAULT NO.57

Pitch and run – where's the run?

X There can be no doubt that working on your pitching technique and developing a good feel for the distance you fly the ball will quickly benefit your game. But don't fall into the trap of relying totally on that high-flying shot. There are times when throwing the ball up into the air just isn't a good idea. If you have a strong wind into your face, or behind you, for example, or if the greens are firm and you have plenty of room to work with, hitting a lower, controlled pitch-and-run shot is often a much more sensible option. However, trying to hit a shot firmly with a lofted club and getting it to run can prove difficult to execute if you impart too much spin on the ball.

The danger is hitting down too steeply. Even though you may produce the desired low trajectory, the excessive backspin placed on the ball will cause it to check up short of the hole. Then you find yourself caught up in a vicious circle: because you are coming up short so often, you begin to hit the shot harder. Which imparts even more backspin, and so it goes on. Basically, any control you have over how far the ball will run is lost.

FIX NO.57

Let the club work around your body

The key here is hitting the shot with overspin, so that the ball 'releases' on landing. To do this, your first move is to **play the ball further back in your stance than on a regular pitch shot**. Using a lofted club – a wedge or 9-iron is fine – lean your weight towards the target, place your hands well ahead of the ball, and **stand almost square to the target**, as opposed to open. That's the first part of the equation taken care of. Now you have to learn to swing the clubhead correctly, so that it **approaches impact on a shallow angle**, thus enabling you to pick the ball almost cleanly off the turf.

Your set up will allow you to work the clubhead away from the ball more inside the target line than normal. Then, as your body turns through the shot, **encourage your right arm to turn over your left**, thus releasing the clubhead. Imagine you are hitting a mini-draw; **feel that the toe of the club is closing as you strike the ball**, and keep both the backswing and the follow-through reasonably short.

Through all of this, **keep your grip pressure light** to encourage the club to release. Any attempt to hit 'at' the ball will only steepen your angle of approach, and induce backspin. Finally, practise tossing a ball underarm, trying to make it run as much as possible – almost like bowling. To do that, **your right arm has to rotate and release**, which is exactly the action you must strive to achieve on these pitch-and-run shots.

CHAPTER 8
Bunker Play

"There is a definite art to
successfully escaping the sand. But
with the right understanding and a little
practice, you might be pleasantly
surprised how quickly you can
improve your bunker technique, and
thus like the tour players, make the
sand your friend as opposed to
being your enemy."

FAULT NO.58

Struggling to escape the sand?

X For too many amateurs, bunkers represent a formidable obstacle. Often it is a simple misconception that creates the problem. Well-worn phrases like 'explosion shot', 'blast it out', and 'take the club outside and cut across the ball' can be particularly misleading, conjuring up images which do little to enhance the chances of a successful escape.

It's easy to fall into the trap (excuse the pun) of trying to exert too much force. I often see players who are guilty of swinging too violently, the result being that the club usually enters the sand at too steep an angle, taking too much sand. Inconsistency results. In the worst cases the ball is either left in the sand, or you over-compensate on the downswing, don't take any sand at all, and thin the ball over the green.

Remember, the greenside sand shot is unique in that it is the only one in golf where the club never makes contact with the ball. The clubhead strikes the sand, and the ball then rides out of the bunker atop a divot of sand. The secret to achieving this, of course, lies in producing a swing that removes a consistent, narrow cut of sand from beneath the ball.

FIX NO.58

Understand basic bunker technique

Assuming you have a good lie, always take your sand-wedge from a greenside bunker. With its heavily flanged sole, your objective through impact is for the club to '**bounce**' through the sand, and not dig uncontrollably. Striking the sand in this way enables you to control the depth of the divot of sand you take – and thus the distance you hit the ball. **The key is to keep the clubface open throughout the swing** – and to do that, the way you form your grip is vital. Remember, **always open the clubface a few degrees and then take your grip**. Gripping normally and simply turning the clubface into an open position just does not work.

With that in mind get in the practice bunker and follow these rules: **Set your body approximately 30 degrees open in relation to the target line** (weight evenly distributed), and position the ball forward in your stance. Now **flex your knees** and shuffle your feet into the sand for a firm footing. **Focus on a spot two or three inches behind the ball** – that's where you want the back edge of the club to enter the sand. **Swing the club smoothly back along the line of your toes**, and let your wrists hinge naturally in response to the weight of the clubhead. **As you start the downswing**, **re-route the club along the target line**, so that you encourage a shallow angle of attack – it should feel like your swing has a slight loop in it as you change direction from backswing to downswing. **Accelerate the clubhead through the sand towards the target** – don't quit on it. Rehearse this without a ball at first, and listen to the sound you make – believe it or not you can actually hear a good bunker shot.

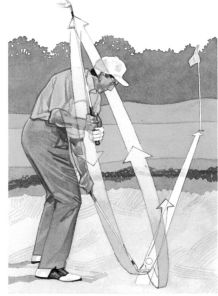

FAULT NO.59

Bunkers – no feel for distance

X Whatever your handicap, the first priority from a greenside bunker is getting out first time. Only when you are confident of achieving that should you start thinking about knocking the ball close to the flag.

Many of the problems that I see players having from bunkers – and I'm talking particularly about those of you who are able to get the ball out but rarely get it close to the flag – seem to result from a basic lack of understanding when it comes to controlling how far the ball will travel from sand. On longer shots they try to hit closer to the ball and swing excessively down into the sand. The result? Plenty of aggression, but little forward momentum. The player takes such a deep chunk of sand that it's all but impossible for the ball to fly very far. Predictably, the shot ends up miles short.

Short shots are similarly mistreated. Here, the tendency appears to be to try to take more sand than normal with a short, jabby stroke. Where and how far the ball goes following that line of reasoning is anyone's guess.

Fix No.59

Control the acceleration

To achieve consistent results from a greenside bunker, you must understand that **virtually every shot you play requires that you take a similar amount of sand** – a slice about 6 inches long and 3 inches wide is your objective. Given a reasonable lie, aim to make contact with the sand a couple of inches behind the ball – that's a good guide. Then, to determine the distance you hit the ball, **the only variable you need to worry about is the speed at which you swing the club to displace the sand**, thus controlling the force with which the ball is thrown onto the green. Slow your tempo for short shots; quicken it to hit the ball further.

To regulate the speed at which you release the club, **aim to make the same length backswing on every shot**, **but vary the length of your follow-through**. **A consistent-length backswing gives you the smooth rhythm you need**; controlling your follow-through determines the amount of acceleration of the clubhead through impact. **Make a shorter follow-through for a short shot, a higher finish for a longer shot**. Work on this acceleration factor when you practise – you'll find that your judgement of distance improves dramatically.

FAULT NO.60

No touch on short, delicate, shots

Few shots in golf demand greater touch and clubhead control than this one – the short greenside bunker shot to a pin that is cut only a few feet from the edge of the trap. To get close requires a soft 'splash', so that the ball pops up quickly and yet lands softly before trickling on towards the flag.

Generally speaking, the problems that you will typically encounter are two-fold: (1) you can either decelerate the clubhead into the sand, leaving the ball in the bunker, or, more commonly (2) strike the ball too firmly, with the result that the ball runs way past the hole. Obviously, the solution involves learning to make a positive swing, and yet produce a shot that flies a short distance and lands softly. And that's not an easy combination.

FIX NO.60

Make an aggressive splash

In common with the majority of the bunker shots that you play, this one requires that you aim to take a shallow cut of sand from beneath the ball. But to encourage a swing that will enable you to produce the necessary flight and soft landing, you need to make one or two subtle adjustments at the set up.

First, **widen your stance**. **Stand a little more open and further away from the ball than you would normally**. **Lower your hands**, too, and **place them behind the ball** so that you effectively add loft to the clubface. Remember, you want to maximize the effective loft on the clubface so that you can release the club aggessively through impact, creating a splash of sand, and yet only have the ball travel a short distance.

As you swing the club back, **try to 'cup' your left wrist** as much as possible so that you exaggerate its open position. Then, stabilizing your swing with a **solid lower body action**, accelerate the club into the sand, **sensing that your right hand works under the left** so that the face of the club is looking skyward as it passes beneath the ball. It will probably feel wristy, which is fine as long as the clubface stays open.

Finally, as you turn to complete what ought to be a fairly short follow-through, **check that you are looking directly at the clubface**. You might be shocked at just how much finesse you actually possess.

FAULT NO.61

No adjustment for a sloping lie

X Negotiating a sloping lie in a greenside bunker is never an easy task. But you can make those awkward situations all the more difficult to cope with if you fail to adjust your address position to suit the slope you are on. For example, if, on a downslope, you set up to the ball as if you were going to play a shot from a flat lie – ie. with your shoulders relatively level **(1)** – the tendency is that you will swing the club away too low on the backswing and then hit up on the ball as you come through. What happens then is that you either catch the sand too far behind the ball, or miss the sand completely and hit the shot too cleanly.

A failure to adjust on an upslope can be just as costly **(2)**. Here, a regular set-up position (in which you will appear to be leaning into the slope) will tend to produce a swing that delivers the club at much too steep an angle into the sand behind the ball. The clubhead will be driven directly into the sand, making it difficult to achieve any forward momentum. Indeed, in many cases the ball will not go the desired distance, and may even be left in the bunker.

(1)

(2)

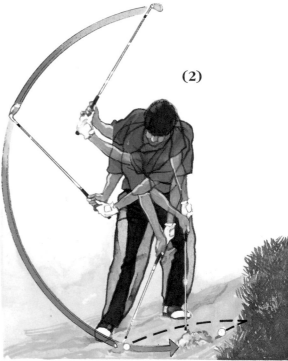

FIX NO.61

Pre-set the correct mechanics at address

✓ **The key to playing from any sloping lie is to adjust your address position to suit the slope as far as possible**. When you set up to the ball, **try to position your body approximately perpendicular with the slope**, and **get your shoulders as parallel with the slope as possible**.

On a downslope, getting that set-up involves supporting most of your weight on your left side and really flexing your left knee until your body is correctly angled down the slope **(1)**. Widen your stance, shuffle your feet into the sand for stability and play the ball back in your feet. In the swing, keep your lower body action to a minimum, and control the club with your hands and arms. **Cock your wrists to swing the club up relatively steeply**, then **concentrate on chasing the clubhead down the slope and through the sand**. Make a fairly short follow-through, and allow for the fact that the ball will come out low and roll.

On the upslope, adjusting your position at address requires that you place most of your weight on your right side. Play the ball forward in your stance and choke down on the grip **(2)**. Then, **feeling the right side of your body set low to get your shoulders parallel with the slope**, **trace the contour of the slope as you swing the club back and through**, **aiming to accelerate the clubhead up and through the sand to a high finish**. This time the ball will tend to fly high and stop very quickly, so aim for the top of the flag.

(1)

(2)

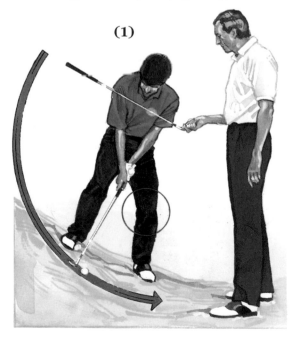

FAULT NO.62

Unable to cope with the buried lie

X There are few things worse in golf than just missing the green with a well-struck approach shot, only then to find that your ball has plugged – or semi-plugged – itself in a greenside bunker.

Of course, situations like this are sent to test your character. The question is, how do you react? Consider the following scenarios:

Act 1: On finding your ball buried in the sand, you moan with self-pity. Clenching your sand-wedge, you smash down into the sand as hard as you possibly can. After the dust clears, you find that the ball has moved about a foot.

Act 2: Upon discovering your misfortune, you reluctantly accept the fact that, in golf, you're not always going to get a good lie, and set about figuring out the best way to get the ball safely out of the bunker and onto the green.

Clearly, the former approach is unlikely to benefit your score. So let's see what we can do about accepting the situation as it is, thus minimizing the damage, and saving strokes.

Fix No.62

Close the face, bury the clubhead

When the ball is plugged, the method you must use is one that encourages a **digging action**, utilizing the sharper leading edge of your wedge or sand-wedge.

To do that, first **square up your stance and place more of your weight on your left foot. Play the ball back in the middle of your feet**, and then give some thought to the position of the clubface. Given normal circumstances, you would open the face and then grip the club, but when the ball is plugged, grip the club as you would do normally, and then **toe the clubface in slightly**, so that it points to the left of the target.

To execute the shot, **pick the club up with a noticeably sharp wrist break** (thus creating the necessary steepness in your backswing) and then, using plenty of right hand, swing the clubhead smoothly into the sand, aiming to make contact just behind the ball – there should be very little follow-through to speak of.

The key is to **leave the clubhead in the sand**. As it meets with the resistance of the sand at impact, the closed clubface you introduced at address will be forced open, sending the ball straight to your target. Finally, bear in mind that from a buried lie, the ball will inevitably fly with overspin, so make sure that you allow for plenty of roll when the ball hits the green. Remember, **your objective is to get the ball out**.

FAULT No.63

Bunkers – absolutely no clue

Some golfers – especially those whose mind is intent purely on hitting the ball – find it a very difficult proposition when faced with a situation where they now have to hit behind the ball in order to be successful with the shot. In fact, some players are so terrorized at the prospect of escaping from the sand that they fear they will never get the ball out. Their confidence is zero, and trying to play the shot with the conventional type of technique – ie. cocking the wrists and taking a shallow cut of sand with an accelerating swing through impact – can be demoralizing.

In severe cases such as this, I feel I have no option but to go straight to plan B with a pupil. Certainly, the key to consistent bunker play lies in repeating a swing that removes a shallow divot of sand, and, fortunately, there's more than one way of achieving that goal. So if the prospect of an alternative solution appeals to you, here's plan B.

FIX NO.63

A one-piece, wristless action

☑ True, plan B is rather unorthodox. But believe me, it's effective. To begin, **hold the clubface square and aim a couple of inches behind the ball**. Now, **take a slightly wider stance than normal, play the ball in the centre of your feet** and **align your body square** – and not open – to the target line. Only a little different so far – but here's the punchline: I want you to swing the club back and through **sensing that you do not cock the wrists. Focus on the triangle that is formed between your arms, shoulders and chest**, and **swing the club and your firm wrists back in one piece on a fairly straight line until you feel that the club is approximately parallel to the ground**. Then, **to make your downswing, keep your lower body passive**, and simply **swing the triangle back through impact and on towards the target**.

The key to this method is to forget about using your wrists and **keep the angle of the approaching clubhead shallow into the sand**. As the clubhead accelerates through impact you can actually hit anywhere from one to four inches behind the ball and it will still come out. So your margin for error is greater than ever.

To hit the ball further you simply swing your arms and rotate your chest more aggressively. Do this for a while, gain a little confidence and who knows, you may even be able to then adopt the regular technique as explained in Fix 58.

CHAPTER 9
The Game in General

"As a teacher I recognize the fact that golfers need to be skilful in all areas of the game in order to shoot low scores, and also that instruction has to be tailored to meet, not only the specific needs of each individual, but the ever-changing demands a typical round of golf throws up."

FAULT No.64

A problem with fairway traps

X This is cruel, I know, but it often amuses me to watch an amateur player go through the process of first weighing up and then playing a shot from a fairway bunker. You can see the determination to hit the ball as far as possible written across his face – although not always with the proper technique in mind. The temptation to 'go for it' is just too great for him to bare, which is why it often takes him more than one attempt to get the ball out.

The point that I'm making, of course, is that not enough players walk into a fairway bunker with 'safety' first and foremost in their mind. Bunkers are a hazard; you must learn to treat them with respect, and make it your priority to get the ball back in play. Consider your options: How is the ball lying? How high is the front lip? How soft is the sand? What other hazards lie within range? These are the questions that need answering before you select the appropriate club and attempt to play.

Fix No.64

Stop ... look ... evaluate ... act

This is a time to be totally realistic about your capabilities. Take a moment to evaluate the situation. **Study the lie of the ball**, feel the texture of the sand through your feet and **note the severity of the lip of the bunker**. Try to **visualize the shot that will put you back in play** with the minimum risk; **play the shot you know you can hit**, rather than one you might be able to get away with. I'm inclined to suggest that you never attempt to use anything more than a 4-iron, no matter how far it is to the green. A fairway wood is asking for trouble.

So, assuming you have a reasonable lie, **you have to at all costs hit the ball first before the sand** – even a thin shot can end up in good shape. You want to encourage a 'sweeping' type motion, one which enables you to pick the ball off the sand. You should **focus your eyes on the top half of the ball** to help promote this. Obviously your balance is a major factor in determining your ability to hit a good shot, so shuffle your feet into the sand until you feel you have a solid base. Then **roll your feet inward slightly** for even more stability. Play the ball back in your stance and **choke down on the grip** a little, too.

To encourage the desired shallow sweeping motion through impact, swing the club back on more of an inside path than normal. Control the swing with your arms and shoulders – the less active your legs are, the more chance you have to hit the ball solidly. Above all, **concentrate on 'staying down'** on the shot through impact, and always **swing to a balanced finish**.

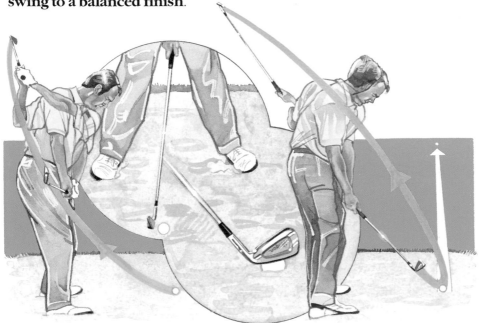

FAULT NO.65

Uphill and downhill battles

X If you play most of your golf on a relatively flat course, and then visit a hilly course, a sloping lie – either uphill or downhill – can be a shock to the system. Handling these situations is all part of being a complete golfer. These tricky lies basically test the versatility of your set-up position. But they also test your knowledge of projectile physics.

Let me explain what I mean. Whenever you play off an uphill or downhill lie, the trajectory of the shot will be determined, not only by the loft on the clubface, but by the launch angle that is created at the set -up. If you are playing off an uphill slope, for example, your launch angle is effectively tilted up, and so loft will be added to your shot. As a result, the ball will tend to fly much higher than normal, but not travel as far forward. On a downhill lie, the opposite is true. Then, your launch angle is diminished, and the slope effectively subtracts loft off the clubface. So no matter what club you use, the ball flies with a lower trajectory than normal, and usually travels further.

DO YOU—
PLAY HERE
OFTEN?

Fix No.65

Work with the laws of physics

For both situations, the rule of thumb for hitting solid shots is to **set your body as perpendicular to the slope as possible**. Fighting the slope will only produce poor results.

Let's tackle the uphill lie first. Think about your club selection. Remember, **the upslope tends to produce a higher-flying shot** than normal. Take that into account. Where the distance you have to cover would normally call for a 6-iron, take a 5-iron, and so on.

On the upslope, set yourself perpendicular and play the ball forward in your stance. With this slope you have to avoid swaying down the slope on the backswing; and then on the downswing, you must force yourself to shift as much weight to your left side as possible.

On a downhill lie, **use a more lofted club than normal**, place the ball back in your stance, and keep a little more of your weight on your right foot (keeping it there should stop you swaying toward the target). To ensure you make as solid a contact as possible, **stay down with the shot** and chase the clubhead down the slope. For both these shots, to assist your balance, put more emphasis on swinging your hands and arms, and less on turning your body.

 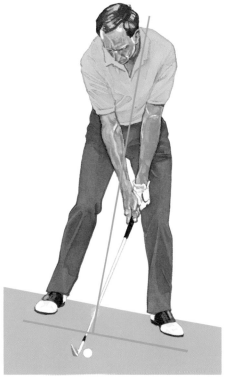

FAULT NO.66

Sidehill problems

X Just as uphill and downhill lies can be a problem, so can sidehill lies (where the ball is either above or below the level of your feet). The point to remember is that your swing is only as reliable as the foundation upon which it is based, so your first task is to make certain adjustments at the set-up that enable you to swing with complete control.

Sadly, such careful pre-shot consideration is rare. Too many players set up to play a ball from a sloping lie as if nothing is different, which is why they usually end up playing their next shot from an even more tricky spot.

Ultimately, of course, the skill that is required to play these shots consistently well comes with practice. But in order for that practice to be effective, you must first understand the physical effects these slopes have, not only on the shape of your swing, but on the subsequent behaviour of the ball in flight.

FIX NO.66

Compensate for the slope at address

The first point to note is that **the ball will tend to move in the direction of the slope – ie. a ball above the level of your feet will tend to fly from right-to-left; one below the level of your feet will move from left-to-right.**

Let's start with the ball above the level of your feet. The slope here will tend to force your weight back toward your heels during the swing. To counter that, **grip down the shaft, stand a little closer to the ball** than normal, and **keep your weight on your toes.** In making these adjustments, your posture will tend to be fairly upright, causing your arms to swing more around your body than normal on a **markedly flatter plane.** The result is a severely in-to-out attack on the ball that creates right-to-left spin, **so aim more to the right** when you take aim.

Conversely, a ball below the level of your feet has just the opposite effect. Your swing will tend to be more upright than normal, and the ball will fly from left-to-right through the air – so aim further left. This time the slope tends to pull your weight forward onto your toes, so take a wider stance than normal and **settle your weight back on your heels. The key is to get 'down' to the shot** without toppling forward. Hold the club as close to the top of the grip as possible, and **flex your knees** until the clubhead rests behind the ball.

Experience will soon teach you that playing these trouble shots is made a good deal easier if you swing within yourself. Keeping your right foot on the ground through impact is one way to encourage making a smooth swing. Try it.

FAULT NO.67

Lack of thought in the rough

X A positive attitude is undoubtedly a great asset to take out onto the golf course, but at the same time you must always be realistic about your capabilities.

Take your strategy in the rough, for example. Generally speaking, the rough defines any part of the golf course which has been specially prepared – or in severe cases simply left as nature intended – to penalize your stray shots. Naturally, the object of the game is to keep the ball on the short grass. But when you do depart the straight and narrow – and no matter how good your swing is you will – it's important that you give careful consideration to your means of recovery.

In my experience, caught in the rough, too many players think only in terms of firing a miraculous recovery to make up for their previous poor effort. Too many shots are wasted through sheer recklessness. Having said that, there are, however, depending on the state of the lie, ways in which you can make a good recovery.

Fix No.67

Assess the situation

☑ **'Where do I want to be playing my next shot from?'** Make this your overriding thought as you survey any shot from the rough. Opt for the recovery that falls well within your capabilities – play the percentage game. For a standard recovery from the rough, choke down on the club, place the ball back in your stance, pick the club up sharply and, with a three-quarter-length swing, accelerate the clubhead through the grass. (Use anything from a sand-wedge to a 5-iron, depending on the severity of the rough. Just make sure you get the ball back in play.)

Now for a couple of fancy shots. If the ball lies in shortish rough, and you need to hit it high to a green, place the ball forward in your stance, **open the clubface** (the grass tends to wrap around the hosel and close the clubface through impact) **and sweep the clubhead through the ball. Let your right hand do most of the work.** If your goal is to hit the ball as far as you can out of the rough, ie. a 2nd shot at a par-5, use more of a punching action. **Move the ball back in your stance, shift your hands and weight forward, keep the clubface square or slightly closed, and make a three-quarter-length swing**, aiming to **lead your left hand into the ball** ahead of the clubface. **Keep your weight left throughout**, and make your follow-through short. **Don't allow the hands to cross over.** Because grass gets caught between the clubface and the ball, no backspin is imparted, and so the ball will run much farther than normal. This is commonly known as a 'flier'.

FAULT NO.68

Fighting the wind

X Playing in the wind adds a unique and invigorating dimension to the game, and ultimately coping with ever-changing conditions is as much a mental challenge as a physical one. Agreed?

Unfortunately, not everyone sees it that way. With the hint of a breeze, too many players get themselves into a poor frame of mind before they've even set foot onto the first tee. These are the players who tend to fight the wind, rather than work with it. They fail to adjust their personal par to take account of the effect the wind has on the ball. When it takes them three shots to reach a short par-4, they get frustrated. They try to hit the ball too hard, and inevitably lose their rhythm. Never does it occur to them that everyone suffers in windy conditions. So the scores generally are higher. It's the way in which you re-think your strategy that counts.

FIX NO.68

Accept the challenge

On a blustery day, make a commitment before stepping out onto the course. **Promise yourself that you will try to swing smoothly.** This way, you will maximize your distance and accuracy simply by focusing on hitting the ball solidly out of the middle of the clubface.

Once you have that game-plan fixed in your mind, take advantage of anything that may help you gauge the strength and direction of the wind, ie. looking at the flags on the greens, throwing grass up in the air, and for a more accurate assessment, checking the tree-tops.

Now it's really a case of trying to assess what effect the wind will have on the flight of the ball, ie., is it a one or two club wind or how far to the left or right do I aim?

When confronted with a head wind or tail wind, **make allowances simply by taking more club into the wind and less club downwind. For the much more difficult crosswind shots, pick a point where you feel you need to start the ball** in order for it to finish on your final target, and then concentrate on making a smooth swing to that point. If your judgment is accurate, the wind will blow the ball back on course – the general rule is, **use the wind to shape your shots, don't fight it**. Experience playing in windy conditions will teach you to become a competent wind player – so above all, enjoy the challenge.

FAULT NO.69

Exaggerated changes for fades and draws

X There are times when being able to 'work' the ball from right-to-left, or left-to-right, can be extremely useful – when the flag is tucked behind a bunker, for example. Also, to achieve the maximum distance with your tee shot around a dogleg, fashioning a stroke to suit the shape of the hole is both a satisfying and rewarding art.

The danger, however, is exaggerating the changes in the set-up that are necessary to fade or draw the ball. There's no need to aim way right, close the clubface, strengthen your grip, swing back inside the line and roll your hands through impact just to draw the ball **(1)**. And you don't have to aim left, open the clubface, weaken your grip, take the club back outside the line and cut across the ball through impact, just to get the ball to move gently from left-to-right, either **(2)**.

In either case, if you make such exaggerated changes in your set-up, you'll end up hooking and slicing the ball. Which of course defeats your original objective of enhancing your control.

(1) **(2)**

Fix No.69

Simple changes to shape the shot

First, let me stress that working the ball is really for the better player, and that it requires practice. For this fix, I define a draw or a fade as a shot that only curves up to 30 feet in the air. So the changes you need to make to your set-up are subtle, to say the least.

To hit a draw – align your body a little to the right of your target, and **aim the clubface where you want the ball to start** (in this case to the right of your target). Place the ball two ball-width's further back in your stance than normal – in effect, the clubface is open at address. Now make a normal swing along the line of your body, but as you approach the ball, feel as if your left arm is rotating counter-clockwise (left hand knuckles to the ground). In so doing, **the clubface will be closing on the ball** as you swing through impact. **Finish with your left elbow down close to your body (1)**. The spin that you impart, as a result of aiming right and closing the clubface, will cause the ball to move from right-to-left through the air.

To play the fade, set up with your body **aimed only a touch left of your target**, and again **aim the clubface where you want the ball to start** – ie. to the left – and place the ball two ball-width's forward in your stance (the clubface is, in effect, closed). Now, swing back along the line of your slightly open stance, but through impact feel that you are trying to open the clubface; **feel that your right arm is working under your left** (knuckles of the left hand to the sky). This opening motion of the clubface, combined with your open stance, will impart the desired left-to-right spin. **Finish high with your left elbow in a 'chicken-wing' position (2).**

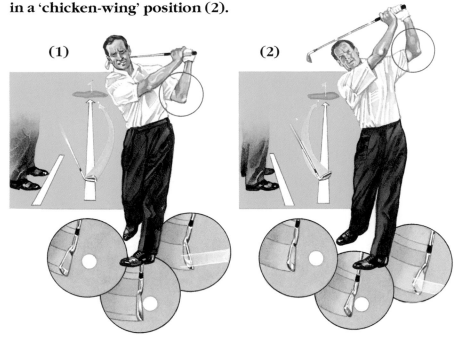

(1) (2)

Fault No.70

Intimidated by fairway woods/long irons

X If you play most of your golf on a relatively long course, you'll certainly appreciate the importance of mastering the long irons and fairway woods in terms of determining your ability to score well. Most club golfers who hit the ball average distances will be required during the course of a round to hit a lot of fairway woods and 3- or 4-irons. These clubs are problematical for a lot of golfers.

The trouble is, these longer-shafted, relatively straight-faced clubs make many players nervous. Nine times out of ten, the shot is struck poorly for the simple reason that the player feels he must hit under the ball or 'lift' it up into the air. How can a club with such minimal loft possibly get the ball airborne without a little help? Over-anxiousness breeds a short, quick, nervy swing. The backswing is rarely completed, rhythm is poor and most shots are 'quit' on as the player falls onto his back foot in a valiant attempt to hoist the ball into the air. Inevitably, the shots tend to do just the opposite.

FIX NO. 70

'Complete' and 'clip'

A fairway wood and long iron contact the ball almost right at the bottom of the swing arc, as opposed to a short or mid-iron where the ball is struck as the clubhead is descending, and a tee-shot, where contact is made as the clubhead begins its ascent. The turf is therefore barely scraped by the clubhead – hardly any divot is taken – and the feeling you should have is that you 'clip' the grass.

To achieve this consistently, the ball should be positioned just back of where a tee shot is addressed. Then, in the swing itself, make a real effort to **complete** your backswing smoothly by turning your back to the target and getting your left shoulder under your chin **(1)**.

If you can satisfy these conditions then the chances are that you'll transfer your weight correctly and make the most effective use of a good body pivot. **From this fully 'wound' position**, simply **focus on watching the ball, staying down with the shot** through impact **(2)**, and **swinging all the way through to a full and balanced finish (3)**.

Make some practice swings with a long iron or fairway wood, and try to just **clip** the top of the grass as you accelerate through 'impact'. Then trust that same sweeping action with a ball in front of you. Try not to concern yourself with the act of 'hitting' the ball up into the air; just let the ball get in the way of a free-wheeling swing.

FAULT NO.71

Tee shots – lack of distance

X Length off the tee – combined obviously with some accuracy – is a huge advantage to take out onto the course; it sets you up to shoot lower scores. Unfortunately I see many amateurs who fail to maximize their distance with the driver. The reason? Usually a faulty set-up.

To hit a long, high-flying tee shot which rolls upon landing, it is necessary to create an accelerated sweeping motion with the clubhead through impact – one which strikes the ball on the upswing. The tendency I see, however, is for players to address their tee-shots with a driver just as if they were preparing to strike a mid iron – ie. with their weight evenly distributed, the ball back in the stance and their hands forward.

Far from producing the desired upward strike through impact, this type of set-up position promotes a poor turn and weight transfer, little or no extension in the backswing and a steep, downward angle of attack on the ball in the downswing. The result is a very weak, glancing blow on the ball, and, of course, a tremendous loss of power. Topped, smothered and skied shots are common (scuff marks on the top of the driver are a sure sign of this problem).

FIX NO.71

Set up for the long ball

✓ The following adjustments to your address position should be relatively easy to make, and will quickly improve the quality of the strike, the trajectory of your drives and of course, your distance:

• **Tee the ball a little higher than normal**, and play it forward in your stance, opposite the instep of your left foot.

• **Widen your stance slightly**, and settle at least 60 per cent of your weight on your right side. **Your head and your hands should be placed slightly behind the ball.**

• **Maintain a light grip pressure**, relax your body and don't ground the clubhead – hover it slightly above the turf.

Combined, these adjustments will make it a lot easier for you to **make a full and free shoulder turn, create a wide arc** and get your body **fully turned behind the ball** at the top of your swing. You should be aware of an increase in the amount of coil that you create which will then enable you to move back to the left side and accelerate the club through impact with a more **powerful ascending, sweeping motion**. Keep your head back (hit up the back of the ball) and attempt to sweep the ball away without removing the tee-peg.

Work on this procedure on the practice range. Pretty soon you may well be playing a game with which you are not familiar.

FAULT NO.72

Ladies – too flexible to coil?

X I liken the backswing to loading a catapult – the further you stretch it back, the greater the resistance you meet until eventually it must be released. On the backswing, the more coil and torque you create, the more power and speed you gain to deliver the clubhead into the back of the ball. Understanding just how to create that resistance, is a stumbling block for many women golfers. Because they are so much more flexible than the men, they often find it difficult to contain their lower body motion, and as a result fail to create the resistance in their hips and knees that is necessary to wind their upper body correctly.

The exaggerated position you see my wife, Kelly, demonstrating here is typical of the problems many women golfers get into. As the left heel comes off the ground, the knees can be seen to almost touch, and the hips turn nearly as far as the shoulders. The upper body raises up (rather than turning behind the ball), causing the arms to lift severely. A poor turn and inadequate weight transfer is the inevitable result, characterized here by a noticeable overswing. This poor backswing motion causes the clubhead to decelerate on the way down to the ball, producing weak shots.

Fix No.72

Create resistance

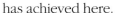 In every good swing the lower body has to provide a certain resistance to the coiling motion of the upper body. A great way for women to create that resistance is to **practise with your left foot turned out** as far as you can comfortably get it. This will serve to restrict your lower body motion and help you to appreciate the **sensation of turning and winding your upper body against the resistance of your lower half**. Try it. Your swing will feel **shorter** and more **compact**. You will sense a turning with your upper body – as opposed to the lift. Look at the position Kelly has achieved now: note the restricted hip turn, the improved weight transfer, and see how the gap between her knees has been maintained.

This whole motion is designed to get you to accelerate the club with much more speed through impact, giving your shots much more **'zip'**. Once you get used to this feeling, gradually return your left foot to a more orthodox position. But remember the importance of a solid lower body action.

Also being so flexible, many women do not actually need to lift their left heel in making a backswing. So, if you are suffering with an ineffective leg action, make a conscious effort to keep your left heel planted on the ground. That will enable you to get into the dynamic position that Kelly has achieved here.

FAULT NO. 73

Ladies – no power

This is a problem that I know confounds many women golfers. Although you are regularly complimented on the fact that you have a 'nice looking swing', you don't seem to be able to hit the ball very far. In fact, no matter how hard you try to create power, there is little noticeable difference in the distance that you hit any of your longer clubs – ie. 3-iron, 4-iron and fairway woods all tend to go the same distance. Your swing may well be elegant to look at, but when, for example, you struggle to reach par-4's in two or three shots, and have no chance of getting on a par-3 in one shot, that is of little compensation.

Sure there's a strength factor to take into account. But I find that many ladies lose power because they fail to use the proper wrist action during the swing – almost 'stiff-arming' their shots. Consequently they lose mega-distance with the long clubs.

Fix No.73

Thoughts on creating speed

✓ To improve your wrist action and help you to create more clubhead speed and power, **first change to a pure two-handed grip**. Simply place your right hand below the left hand on the grip and position the club in the fingers of both hands. This will give you a more powerful feeling by placing more emphasis on your stronger right hand.

Now work on this drill to improve your wrist action: (1) take a short iron and stick a tee into the end of the grip; (2) making half-swings, swing the club freely back and forth, cocking and un-cocking your wrists so that the tee points directly down at the ground, both in the backswing and again in the follow-through. In other words, **cock your wrists** as you swing the club back, **un-cock** them as you swing the club down and through impact, then **re-cock** them up on the follow-through.

Working on this action in conjunction with the correct body motion will help you to appreciate just how powerful the hingeing of the wrists can be. (3) Move on to hitting some shots off a tee with your 'mini-swing'. Take a 7-iron and **see how far the ball flies with little effort**. (4) Finally, pick up your driver, turn it upside down and hold the head. Make some swings. Focus on the wrists and really **try to swish the grip-end of the club through impact** as loudly as you can. I guarantee that when you go back to hitting normal shots with this correct wrist action you'll shock yourself with all the extra power you have to play with.

FAULT NO.74

Juniors – over-coaching

X There's a fine line between teaching a youngster a few things that he needs to know to get started at golf, and burdening him with a lot of technical advice. I often see well-meaning adults and parents trying to coach children, and of course it's important that you do offer encouragement and a grounding in the fundamentals of the game. But be careful. Without realizing it, you might easily be doing more harm than good.

Junior golfers aren't really interested in detailed theory, so don't fill their heads with it. Too much advice makes them think too hard and they then lose their natural ability to swing at the ball. Their tendency to experiment and learn through a process of trial and error will be seriously threatened. Moreover, they may start to totally focus on 'positioning' the club, rather than simply swinging it – just like Dad. The danger, ultimately, is that they get bored, lose interest, have no fun and give up.

OK, REMEMBER, ANDY. AWAY LOW, SLOW. COCK YOUR WRISTS, TURN YOUR SHOULDERS, MOVE — YOUR WEIGHT ACROSS, WATCH THE BALL FOLLOW THROUGH.

Fix No.74

The bare essentials for young players

If you're involved in junior golf, I suggest that you base the advice you give on the following ideas – then leave the young players well alone!

- **Make sure the clubs they use are suitable**. Heavy, full-length clubs can seriously hamper the development of a junior's swing. See your local professional for advice.

- **Give them an opportunity to watch good players in action**, either at a tournament or on TV. Children are great mimics, and will invariably copy what they see.

- Give them a grip that is suited to returning the clubface squarely to the back of the ball. That means having **at least three knuckles visible on the back of the left hand**, usually with a baseball or ten-finger grip to start with.

- Stress the importance of **aiming at a specific target**.

- In every full swing, keep the theory simple, but encourage them to **watch the ball**, and **brush the grass** both on the way back and on the way through. Get them to focus on **motion** and **swinging the club** through to a full, **balanced finish**.

- **Encourage them to work on their short game**. The touch and feel they develop early in their golfing career will stay with them forever.

- **Teach them the rules and etiquette** of the game, but above all else, **make golf fun** for them. Let them play and compete whenever possible, and eventually seek out a good teaching professional for continued development.

FAULT NO.75

Seniors – loss of mobility and distance

Such is the irony of life. Just as you get to that stage when you have more time on your hands to enjoy your golf, your body renders itself too many over par to play on. You seem to be losing more distance every year and it is difficult to get the old body into motion.

For the majority of golfers, the inevitable result of the ageing process is that they relinquish flexibility, the swing gradually becomes shorter, and they lose a lot of power. The danger then, as your body turn becomes increasingly restricted, is that you make compensations to try and hit the ball solidly, often resulting in a weak release of the clubhead and absolutely no consistency.

Fix No.75

Turning back the years

Fortunately there are ways in which your golf game can be rejuvenated. Regard this as a two-part fix.

(1) Exercise at home – **train for a better body turn**. Hook a broom handle behind your back and hold it in place as you work on **rotating your body to the right** and hold that position for a count of seven. Then **rotate to your left** and do the same. Five minutes a day is enough. Within a couple of months your flexibility – and thus your ability to turn – will have improved tremendously.

(2) Work on your swing. **You need to learn to complete your backswing**, and get the club releasing and accelerating on an inside path back to the ball so that you maximize your distance. To this end, stand with **your feet fairly close together**, then **pull your right foot and right hip back** until your body is in a closed position in relation to the target line. **This will help you turn your right side out of the way on the backswing.** Now, with the ball positioned back in your modified stance, make a swing (raising your left heel and allowing your left arm to bend slightly will enable you to fully complete your backswing). This relaxed position at the top will allow you to move through the ball freely and **use your hands and arms** to snap the clubhead through and strike the ball solidly. A draw should be the result – which will immediately increase your distance. With a little practice and trust in this new free swing, the game will soon become fun again.

FAULT NO.76

The problem with being tall

X It is no coincidence that many of the game's greatest players have been of less than average height. Being very tall is no advantage in golf. Longer limbs only serve to complicate your method; they can often be seen to introduce a great deal of wasted motion, which inevitably leads to an inconsistent strike and a poor shot pattern. In contrast, a short player with a much lower center of gravity will benefit from a greater level of stability, and a significantly wider margin for error in his swing.

But, I hear you say, doesn't being tall widen your arc and so enable you to hit the ball a long way?

Well, yes, to an extent. But clubhead speed without any control causes great inconsistency – while some shots will go far, many more will fly far off line. The shorter golfer will tend to swing more efficiently, maximize his leverage and regularly hit shots out of the middle of the clubface. In other words, he will tend to hit the ball as far as he is physically able more often with control.

FIX NO.76

Making the necessary adjustments

☑ **Correctly fitted clubs are essential** if you want to fulfil your potential as a golfer. Only with clubs that have been measured to suit your physique will you be able to set up to a shot correctly and consistently – a particularly troublesome task for every tall golfer.

With this in mind, question the suitability of your clubs: do you need longer shafts? A more upright lie (especially if you have short arms)? Or thicker grips? If you're in any doubt, see your golf professional.

Now let's focus on your stability. To offset the natural tendency to bend over too much to get down to the ball, you need to **widen your base** and **flex your knees more**. Make the minimum distance between your feet shoulder-width (for a shorter player that's the maximum). This lowers your centre of gravity and helps you maintain your balance. Once you feel reasonably comfortable, **push your hips and knees toward the target slightly, raising the left hip**, thus setting your right side a little lower and further securing the foundation of your swing.

Finally, make a conscious effort to **swing comfortably within yourself** – don't try to smash every shot. Attempt to make no more than a three-quarter-length backswing and always swing to a balanced finish. You already have a naturally wide arc, so achieving a respectable distance is never going to be a problem. Consistency is what you are after. Remember, the woods are full of long hitters – you're better off hitting the ball where the mowers have been!

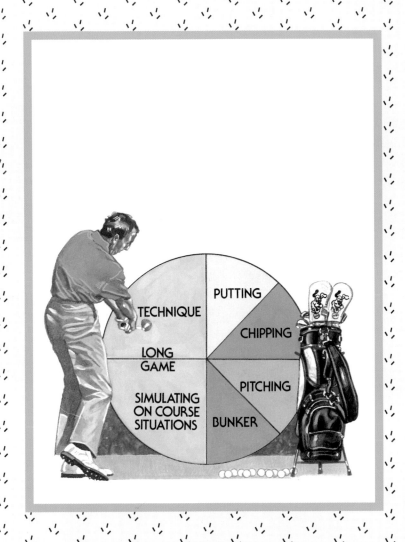

CHAPTER 10
Using your Head

"Once your faults have been fixed
mechanically, the sure route to success
is using the longest of all shots – the
six-inch distance between your ears.
Mentally, applying yourself during the
learning and development stage will
allow you to shoot the lowest
possible score."

FAULT NO.77

Pre-shot routine – what's that?

How would you rate your pre-shot routine? Disciplined? Inconsistent? Downright sloppy? Nonexistent? If I had to pick out just one thing that the top professional players have in common it would be that they all follow a consistent pre-shot routine. Of course they vary – everyone is different. But from the time they pull the club from the bag to the moment they start to swing, their mannerisms follow a well-rehearsed pattern.

First they stand behind the ball and visualize the shot they want to hit. Then they place the club behind the ball and check their aim before settling into a comfortable position. They waggle the club a set number of times to keep their body moving, which also helps them to stay relaxed. Even the time they spend completing this routine is a constant factor on every shot.

For amateurs, however, it's a random process: their method of alignment is haphazard and sloppy, ie. on the tee they spend too much time over the ball; on the fairway, barely a few seconds. Sometimes they waggle the clubhead, sometimes not at all. There's no pattern.

They also don't know when to walk away from a shot and start over again. If something breaks what routine they do have, they may look up to see what happened, but they don't step away from the ball. They just carry on regardless, even though their focus has been broken – and then they wonder why the shot was lousy.

FIX NO. 77

Make hitting good shots a habit

Playing by a set routine is the surest way to guarantee hitting good shots more often. We are creatures of habit, and respond to repetition. Here's an example of a sound, step-by-step approach:

• Stand a few yards behind the ball with your chosen club and look at the target. **Picture the shot** you want to hit; **visualize** how you want the ball to fly, land and finish.

• Walk to the ball and position yourself so that you are approximately parallel to the target line.

• With your feet together, place the clubhead behind the ball so that it looks **squarely** at the target, and adjust your body so that it is exactly parallel.

• Move your left foot to the left and your right foot to the right. This eliminates the need to worry about your ball position. It will be the same every time.

• Look at the target. Gently shuffle your feet – **constant movement is a must**. Then **relax your arms** and waggle the club a few times.

• Take one last look at the target, **sense the shot**, look back at the ball, **exhale** (this helps you to relax) and think of your swing key.

• **Pull the trigger** and swing.

Repeat this over and over, with and without a ball to make it instinctive so that it becomes a part of your overall swing. Follow this plan closely, or modify it to suit your own style of play. **But do it every time**. You'll be pleasantly surprised at how it can improve your game.

FAULT No.78

Under-clubbing, always short

X Stand behind any green for an hour and make a note of how many golfers reach pin-high with their approach shots. Not many, I'll wager. The majority will be short.

It's that old ego problem. Too many golfers have an unrealistic idea of how far they can hit their irons on a regular day-to-day basis. They usually base their choice of club on their very best shot rather than on their average.

Why this obsession about distance? As long as the ball is hit on-line and flies the correct distance through the air, who cares what club you used? Irons are direction clubs, not distance clubs. That's why you have a whole set! Think about it logically: most of the trouble that you will encounter on the golf course – ie. water hazards and bunkers – are to be found short of the green. Failing to take sufficient club is the cardinal error in general course management.

What's more, trying to hit an iron too hard invariably causes you to lose your rhythm. Which causes you to mishit the shot. Which causes you to lose even more distance. Has the penny dropped?

FIX NO.78

Taking extra club = better results

✔ I have already made reference to the importance of rhythm and balance in the golf swing; good players always seem to swing within themselves. They are in control of their actions, and thus maintain control of the clubhead.

One of the reasons they are able to do this so consistently is that they know exactly how far they hit each and every club in the bag (usually with about ten yard increments between irons). So they never have to hit an iron shot too hard. **If they need a little extra distance, they simply take an extra club.** Thus, the first rule of good course management is **know how far you hit your clubs**. Get that information to hand, and make good use of it out on the course.

Be realistic, too. Let's assume the average tour pro' (who plays and practises almost every day and who has a much more efficient swing than you do) hits a 7-iron about 155 yards. That means the chances of you hitting the same club that far, consistently, are slim. Get used to this idea the next time you play. **Make yourself take one more club on every shot.** If you think it's a 7-iron, take a 6-iron. When in doubt, **club up**. In time you'll find that your swing is smoother and you are more likely to hit solid shots to at least pin-high, leaving shorter putts. So your scores should be lower, too.

FAULT NO.79

Too many swing thoughts

X Consider this: you're over the ball, but you're not moving. At least your body isn't. In your mind, however, the wheels are turning at 100 miles an hour. You're tense, and more concerned with the 'how' rather than the 'where' aspect of what you are trying to do.

This scenario is probably more familiar to those of you who take lessons or read golf instruction regularly. Obviously good teaching and well-written articles will help your game if applied correctly in practice, but you must understand that the place to work on improving the mechanics of your swing is away from the course. The idea is that you work on your swing so that when you go out and play, you can forget about it. So set aside time for regular spells of quality practice – that's the only way you'll ever make your swing instinctive on the course.

Some food for thought: the golf swing only takes about a second to complete, and your muscles can only absorb so many commands from your brain before they tighten up. Too many, and your rhythm is likely to be destroyed.

FIX NO.79

Keep it simple on the course

It's very easy to get caught up in the technical aspects of golf, and problems can arise when you try to combine working on your swing with working on your score. The two are not always compatible. Out on the course you must discipline yourself to 'let go' of detailed theory. Flush your mind of unnecessary 'jargon'; carry no more than two swing keys on any swing just to help reinforce your feel – and keep those keys simple.

Think more of swinging the club rather than positioning it. If you are too 'position conscious' your swing will get stilted and jerky. Instead, focus on those swing thoughts that help you sense the swing as a continuous movement, and not as a series of moves which require careful assembly. Good keys, for example, would include: (1) 'complete', and (2) 'swing to the finish'.

These types of thoughts, in general, will help your rhythm by keeping your body and mind relaxed – and in that physical and mental state you will zero in, focus on your target and play your best golf.

Ultimately, all the hard work you put into your game will pay off – your natural instincts will take over and you'll be in what the tour players call 'the zone'.

FAULT No.80

Undisciplined practice

X The old adage that practice makes perfect only applies in golf if you practise with specific goals in mind. Otherwise you will probably be wasting your time. Hitting 150 balls in an hour certainly isn't better than hitting 50 if you hit all those extra balls with no real purpose. It's the 'quality' of your practice that counts.

Structuring your practice time effectively to reflect the importance of the skills that you need out on the course requires a little thought, too. Yet the rational allocation of whatever time is available is not something that I see too much evidence of when the average player heads for the range.

The urge to hammer away with the long clubs – especially the driver – mysteriously takes over. I know it can be fun, but it's not logical, especially when you consider that the short game, so necessary for good scoring, is much more than half the game. Slogging away relentlessly with your driver for an hour, then chipping and putting for ten minutes is really non-productive.

FIX NO.80

This practice will make you perfect!

Sad as it is, there is only so much time you can spend on your golf game, so it is vital that when you do get an opportunity to practise you make the most effective use of your time. Remember, you can **work on drills and exercises at home without a ball** to get certain mechanics down. When you get to the practice area you must **design yourself a schedule** that enables you to work on a lot of different aspects of your game **for technique and scoring**.

Split your time equally between the long and the short game. Let's say you have two hours. Spend the first hour on your long game. In the first half-hour, warm up for five minutes with a wedge to get some feel, then switch to a mid-iron and work purely on swing technique – drills etc. In the second half-hour, **visualize and hit the shots as if you were out on the course**. Note the distances you hit each shot and select specific targets. Work on those speciality shots you might encounter on the course, ie. punch shots, hitting hooks and slices around imaginary trees, uneven lies etc. – you never know when these might crop up.

In the final hour turn your attention to the short game, splitting your time into four segments: **putting, chipping, pitching** and **bunker play**. Remember, **the more realistic you make your practice sessions, the easier you will find it to take your game onto the golf course – where your performance really counts**.

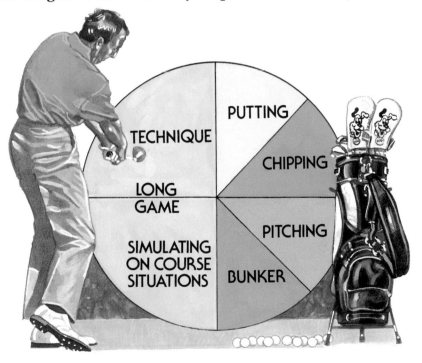

☒ FAULT

☑ FIX

☒ FAULT	PAGE	☑ FIX	PAGE